Contents

Preface

We have chosen to subtitle this book "The Litmus Test" because we believe that the effectiveness with which the education system responds to the needs of Gypsy Roma Traveller families is a good indicator of responsiveness. These communities represent only a small proportion of our population, but they stand out in the national educational indicators. Gypsy Roma Traveller pupils top the league tables in indicators of exclusions, SEN, persistent absence and secondary drop-out. They are also the lowest achieving groups at all Key Stages.

We have tried in this book to explain the complex set of reasons why this is the case, and the equally complex set of actions necessary to address the issue. Both the authors are currently employed running Traveller Education Consortia and one of the reasons we continue to feel stimulated by this area of practice is that there are no easy answers. There is a tradition of moving forward through reflection and dialogue. This book aims to contribute to that debate, and we have tried to present our arguments in a way that will engage the broadest readership. Effective responses to the educational needs of these communities must be informed, flexible and collaborative, and so, as far as possible, we have tried to combine an introduction to readers new to the field, with an analysis of issues which we hope will stimulate those with more experience.

At the time of writing, the future of Traveller Education seems very uncertain, so it is not entirely clear at whom this book should be targeted. Most services have been incorporated into Local Authority school improvement services, alongside Ethnic Minority Achievement and Strategies colleagues. At the same time, the ring-fencing of funding under Children's Services Grant has been withdrawn and, in many areas, the budgets for Traveller Education have been cut. In this context this book has, potentially, a much wider readership. As a mainstreamed service, Gypsy Roma Traveller Education becomes the responsibility of many more people within the authority, and the role of the Traveller Education Support Service may change.

While we have been putting together this book, the National Strategies Gypsy Roma Traveller Achievement programme has been compiling a resource for schools, apparently covering the same ground as this book, and available free. We decided, nevertheless, to continue with our project because we believe the issues are broader and more problematic than the Strategies school improvement approach.

The Strategies document targets schools and focuses on ways in which achievement can be raised. We disagree with nothing in their approach; Gypsy Roma Traveller children learn best in good, flexible inclusive schools, and the inclusion of these communities in integrated national programmes is surely the way forward. But there is a tendency in the current climate to assume that the TESS approach is wrong because of the slow rate of progress made by Gypsy Roma Traveller pupils against national expectations, whether those be attainment, attendance or retention to the end of statutory schooling.

Staff of TESSs share these frustrations, indeed we have always sought, through our professional organisations, to bring them to the attention of policy makers. But the reasons for the limited progress lie beyond the school and the TESS, and we would argue that, in our efforts to appear positive and justify continuing funding, TESSs have tended to underplay the challenges they, and the communities they work with, face.

It is ironic that, at a time when the staff of TESSs are being integrated into other teams within LA services, a national network of virtual headteachers for Looked After Children has been created. There is a recognition that, with very vulnerable children and young people, someone needs to have primary responsibility for safeguarding their educational entitlement in the context of cross-borough and inter-

Traveller Education in the Mainstream:

the Litmus Test

Brian Foster
& Anne Walker

HOPSCOTCH

Published by
Hopscotch, a division of MA
Education,
St Jude's Church, Dulwich Road,
London, SE24 0PB
www.hopscotchbooks.com
020 7738 5454

© 2009 MA Education Ltd.

Written by Brian Foster & Anne Walker

Illustrated by Emma Squire,
Fonthill Creative, 01722 717057

ISBN 978 1 90539 062 5

Every effort has been made to trace the owners of copyright of material in this book and the publisher apologises for any inadvertent omissions. Any persons claiming copyright for any material should contact the publisher who will be happy to pay the permission fees agreed between them and who will amend the information in this book on any subsequent reprint.

Acknowledgements

We would like to start by thanking Liz Rhodes for her warmth and patience in waiting for our rewrites.

We would also like to express our gratitude to Felicity Bonel, Anthea Wormington, Jan Wall and Peter Norton for their supportive critical comments that assisted us in the writing of this book.

We are especially appreciative of our families and in particular David Walker and Hilary Horton for their good humour, patience and forbearance while we neglected them to produce this book.

agency involvement. Whenever Joint Area Review inspections have looked at the work of TESSs, they have been impressed by the way in which services have worked across professional and geographical boundaries in their efforts to make sure all children have the opportunity to reach their full potential.

Referring to Gypsy Roma Travellers as vulnerable groups might appear to denigrate the many families who are successfully raising their children without intervention and support from specialist agencies. Although statistical averages suggest they are vulnerable within the education system, this does not mean that every child and every family is underachieving. Families independently accessing the education system and whose children are benefiting from a broad, balanced and relevant curriculum are the success stories and potential role models. Sadly, because the focus of our work is on raising engagement and achievement, we spend little time with these families and sometimes leave them out of our descriptions. The data-driven approach to education suggests that these children are vulnerable, both in education and most other areas of their lives; but just because the averages suggest vulnerability, it does not mean that every child and family is vulnerable, or that they are vulnerable in all aspects of their lives. Low expectations and stereotyping are a danger, even for those of us who are committed to change.

Gypsy Roma Traveller History Month has provided a wonderful opportunity for a range of Gypsy Roma Travellers to celebrate their histories and identities with a confidence that reminds us of the strength and resilience of the cultures. The fact that we regard them as vulnerable within the education system may reflect more on the unresponsiveness of that system, than on the frailties of the families. The History Month not only undermines the stereotype of cultural fragility, it is also another strategy to help all children to reach their full potential.

Targeted support for the education of Gypsy Roma Travellers may be regarded as something of an anachronism; it should not be necessary if all schools and LA services operated in an inclusive way, if Gypsy Roma Traveller parents understood the potential of education to improve their life chances, if employers and neighbours weren't racist, if cultures weren't conservative.

But just at the moment, that state of affairs does not exist. The rest of the book suggests what we can do about it.

Who are the Gypsy Roma and Traveller Communities?

A number of different communities is included in the generic term Traveller: Romani Gypsies, Irish Travellers, Showmen, Circus people, New Travellers and Bargees. All of these communities have a history of a travelling lifestyle, although their ways of life, histories and cultures vary greatly. In all it is estimated that there are between 200,000 and 300,000 members of the Gypsy Roma Traveller communities in the UK today[1].

Terminology

The term Traveller is acceptable to most of these groups, but many English Gypsies prefer to be called Gypsies. However, Gypsy is a term that can be perceived as having negative connotations and is not acceptable to some. This is often the case with families from Eastern and Central Europe and 'Roma' is the universally preferred term. Fairground people prefer to be called 'Showmen' and Circus people and Bargees have their own traditional occupations and history of planned movement.

Accommodation

Many Gypsies and Travellers live in housing, though exact figures are not known. Others live on local authority or privately owned caravan sites or are resident on their own plot of land. Approximately one-fifth of the non-housed Gypsy and Traveller population have no secure place to stay, and move between unauthorised encampments. Despite this, living in housing is not seen as an ultimate goal by a majority of families. It is estimated that today between 90,000 and 120,000 Gypsies and Irish Travellers live in caravans in England and 2,000 in Wales[2]. Up to three times that number live in conventional housing. The Office of the Deputy Prime Minister commissioned a study into Traveller accommodation and found a shortage of pitches. It was estimated that an additional 4,000 pitches would be needed to ensure that Traveller families had legal pitches and stopping places. Even though many Gypsy people live in housing, it is rarely what they desire, preferring to live in extended family groups and having the opportunity to move nearer to other family members from time to time.

Ethnic groups

Two of the communities are recognised minority ethnic groups under the terms of the Race Relations Act 1976 and the Race Relations (Amendment) 2000. These are the Roma or Romani Gypsies and the Irish Travellers.

All public bodies including schools, local authorities, parish councils and police forces have a statutory general duty to have due regard to the need to:

- Eliminate unlawful racial discrimination

- Promote equality of opportunity

- Promote good race relations between persons of different racial groups.

Children from these groups should be recorded as part of the schools minority ethnic population within the Annual School Census.

Traveller Lifestyles

Travelling people are economic nomads who have always travelled to find work. The most traditional occupations were as farm labourers, blacksmiths, metalworkers, horse dealers and entertainers. In the winter, when travelling was more difficult, families would settle on the outskirts of towns and provide other services such as selling pegs, lace, paper flowers and Christmas wreaths. Fortune-telling was another source of income for the women. Self-employment is one of the defining characteristics of all Travelling people and, while some members of the different communities do take up paid employment, there is still a distinct preference for self-employment. The knowledge that 'portable' skills and trades are highly valued by this community will be of particular importance to those working with and giving careers guidance to adolescents from Traveller communities.

Today occupations are many and varied and include scrap metal dealing, tarmacking, carpet selling, dealing in second hand cars, tree surgery and garden clearance. Other Travellers are turning to the internet as a source of income and are trading on eBay and other sites. New Travellers will have a wide range of occupations, including working in paid employment as well as casual agricultural work, jewellery making, wood carving, music making, providing sound systems, skills in working with solar and wind power and alternative energy.

The mobility of Traveller pupils continues today, though somewhat curtailed and modified by the lack of legal stopping-places.

[1] Common Ground – Equality, good Race Relations and sites for Gypsies and Irish Travellers – A report of the CRE.

[2] Niner "Local Authority Gypsy sites in England. 2002.

Useful Websites

An article on London's Romani Gypsies can be found at: *http://www.untoldlondon.org.uk/news/ART38559.html*

The stories of Gypsy people in Kent can be found at: *http://www.bbc.co.uk/kent/romany_roots/*

The archived CRE website *http://83.137.212.42/sitearchive/cre/gdpract/g_and_t_facts.html*

Roma

Roma are the largest ethnic minority group in Europe and their numbers are growing. There are estimated to be at least 10 million people, with the larger populations in some of the poorest countries of Eastern Europe. In Romania, Macedonia and Bulgaria they comprise more than 10% of the population.

Roma came originally from northwest India around 1,000 years ago. There are no written histories of this period but Romani historians, from analysis of Romanes (the language of Roma), anthropological evidence and blood groups, have concluded they are descended from a multi-ethnic mercenary army. This was assembled by Aryan princes in the Punjab to defend their lands against the expanding Muslim Empire in the area which is now Afghanistan.

Over the next 300 years the Muslim Empire extended westward, carrying the mercenary army and its camp followers with it. Romanes developed from the languages of different groups within the mercenary army, the military patois which enabled them to communicate with each other and the linguistic borrowings from the areas they passed through.

Linguistic detective work suggests the route took them through Upper-Indus Valley, Persia, the Caucuses, Armenia, Byzantium, Greece, the Kingdom of Serbia and into what is now Romania. New research suggests that the army was finally defeated in Armenia in the early fourteenth century. Different Roma groups began to migrate northwards, finally spreading throughout Europe by the sixteenth century. The common Romani language then began to disintegrate into a large number of spoken dialects, influenced by local languages.

Initially Roma were welcomed for their skills and the income that could be made from them, but when economic circumstances changed they were retained by force. In Wallachia and Moldavia Roma were enslaved for 400 years, until the mid-nineteenth century.

Migration patterns of different Roma groups

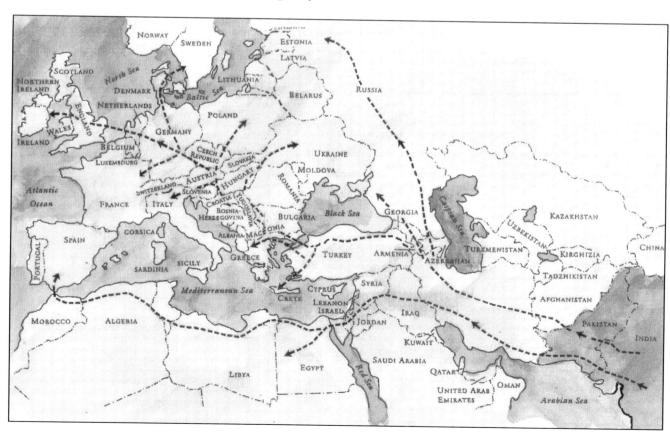

Others who fled north to Poland and Germany experienced such hostility (on the grounds that they were dark-skinned and came from lands now controlled by Muslims) that they headed back to the mountains and forests. Small groups began to migrate into Western Europe, where feudalism was breaking down and there was a living to be made moving between the developing towns and cities. These Roma arrived in the British Isles in the early sixteenth century and were known as Romanichal Gypsies.

Roma experienced prejudice and hostility throughout Europe, involving executions and torture, banishment and forced assimilation. At least 600,000 Roma died in O Parrajmos (the Roma Holocaust), between a quarter and one third of the Roma population in the lands under German occupation. In the post-war era the majority of Roma lived under Communism. Although their freedoms were restricted, and generally their culture was not respected, Roma were entitled, like other citizens, to accommodation, education, health care and employment.

Since the end of the Communist era, many of the newly independent states where the Roma live have embraced nationalism and the free market economy. Anti-Roma prejudice has re-emerged and the high levels of unemployment have disproportionately affected Roma. Poverty is rife and racist attacks common. From the mid 1990s Roma from Kosovo began to come to the UK as asylum seekers, as did many from Poland, the Czech Republic and Slovakia. In 2004 these countries joined the European Union and most families were given leave to remain. In 2007 Romania and Bulgaria joined the EU.

Nationals of the ten Eastern European member states are free to move throughout the EU, but they are not entitled to benefits until they have been in registered work for two years. Nevertheless, poor Roma families, particularly from Romania and Slovakia, have chosen to come to the UK in the hope of improving their circumstances and life opportunities. Roma have found they feel less conspicuous in ethnically diverse towns and cities than in Eastern Europe where they may be the only black minority.

As with all Gypsy Roma Traveller groups, there is great diversity among the Roma communities. Some families have Romanes as a home language, while other families may have lost the use of it. Some may have traditional dress codes and strict rules on gender roles. Most parents who grew up under Communism will be literate and some are highly educated. Most Roma are proud of their identity, although they may use variants of the term Gypsy (for instance Tsiganne, or Tzegeuner) to describe themselves. On the other hand, although most Roma were educated, many attended special schools and ghetto schools, where the quality of education was poor. Czech and Slovak Roma who were relatively well integrated may be quite

reluctant to acknowledge their identity. TESSs have an important role in establishing a dialogue with families to establish what their particular view of culture and identity is.

Most Roma will not have experienced a nomadic life style and would not expect to live on Gypsy Traveller caravan sites; most Eastern European Roma were not nomadic and those who were originally were likely to have been forcibly settled during the 1950s. Nevertheless, extended family responsibilities may require that Roma families return to Eastern Europe from time to time. In common with many other Gypsy Roma Traveller communities, their sense of identity relates to a community rather than a place, and mobility is seen as a solution rather than a problem, and an opportunity rather than a threat.

English Romani Gypsies
Background
This is the largest group in Britain, though precise data is not known due to the lack of census information on Traveller groups. Many English Gypsies also speak Anglo-Romanes; this uses Romani vocabulary within an English grammatical framework.

The first groups of Roma people arrived in Great Britain at the beginning of the sixteenth century, when the community was thought to have originated in Egypt, hence the name 'Gypsy'. Egyptians Acts were passed in 1530, 1554 and 1562 controlling entry to the country and movement. Eventually citizenship was offered to those who assimilated with the local population. In 1596, 106 men and women were condemned to death just for being Roma, but in the event only nine were executed, as the others were able to prove that they were born in England. Although laws were very slowly repealed, the community continued to be subjected to marginalisation and discrimination, being subjected to periodical rounding up and deportation to the British Colonies during the seventeenth and eighteenth centuries.

The Nazis drew up lists of Romani individuals from the UK with a view to internment in the eventuality of a successful invasion of Britain during the Second World War. In Europe it is estimated that between 250,000 and 500,000 Roma people were killed during the Holocaust.

Today, Gypsy people negotiate a complex legislative world. Where they can stop and for how long is regulated through the Criminal Justice and Public Order Act. Planning laws regulate their ability to purchase land and set up private sites. Finding a legal place to live presents challenges that the settled population can only guess at. At the same time, the law requires that all children attend school between the ages of 5 and 16 years. Families can be faced with local authority officials requesting that children are placed in school while others are simultaneously serving eviction orders.

Many traditional cultural practices are still observed, such as keeping different types of washing separate. Often the possessions of the dead are burned or otherwise disposed of.

Useful websites

For more information on the Romani language: *http://romani.humanities.manchester.ac.uk/index.html*

For more information on the Roma People worldwide: *http://www.geocities.com/~Patrin/*

Scottish Travellers

There are two main groups of Scottish Travellers - Lowland Travellers or Romany Gypsies and Highland Travellers. Lowland Travellers share their heritage with English Romanichal Gypsies and Roma, while the Highland Travellers have their roots in northern Europe. However, there are links between the two groups through their cultures and languages, as well as through marriage.

Scottish Lowland Romany Gypsies

Gypsies have been part of Scottish society for at least 500 years. The first official mention of Gypsies in Britain was in 1505, when it was recorded that seven pounds were paid to 'Egyptianis' by King James IV at Stirling. They enjoyed a privileged place in Scottish society until the Reformation, when their wandering lifestyle and exotic culture brought severe persecution upon them.

The 'Ceardannan' or 'Black Tinkers'

The Highland Traveller families are more strongly identified with the native Highland population. Many families carry clan names like Cameron, Stewart, MacDonald and Macmillan. Nobody knows for sure where the Highland Travellers came from. In Gaelic they are known as the 'Ceardannan' (the craftsmen, or 'Black Tinkers') or, as the crofters of the west highland called them, 'The Summer Walkers'. Like Romany Gypsies, Highland Travellers followed a nomadic lifestyle, passing from village to village among the settled population. They would pitch their bow-tents on rough ground on the edge of the village and earn money there as tin-smiths, hawkers, horse-dealers and pearl-fishers. Many found seasonal employment on farms, eg. at berry picking time or during harvest. They also brought entertainment and news to isolated towns and villages.

Certainly Highland Travellers have played a crucial role in preserving traditional Gaelic culture. They have made an outstanding contribution to Highland life through their ancient tradition of singing, story-telling and folklore. Duncan Williamson, a highland Traveller who was famous for his storytelling, died in 2007. His obituary in the Guardian tells an interesting story in itself.

The language they speak is related to the Irish Traveller language called 'Cant' or 'Shelta'.

Useful Websites

http://www.grthm.co.uk/scottish-travellers.php

http://www.scottishtravellered.net/

http://www.guardian.co.uk/news/2007/nov/22/guardianobituaries.obituaries1

Welsh Gypsies

The Romany Gypsies of Wales are known as the Kale and their language is thought to have survived in North Wales until the early part of the twentieth century. The links below give access to a good overview of the history and culture of the Welsh gypsies. The BBC link gives access to an interesting piece of film from 1964.

Useful Websites

http://www.valleystream.co.uk/romany-welsh%20.htm

http://www.bbc.co.uk/wales/eclips/pages/eng_7to14_his_modern_gipsy.shtml

Irish Travellers

The historical origins of Irish Travellers are subject to much debate. Some scholars argue that the Irish Travellers are descended from ancient pre-Celtic tribes of travelling precious metal workers, while others believe that the Travellers were descended from people made homeless during Cromwell's military campaign in Ireland and were later joined by refugees from the Irish famine. It is clear that many were skilled metal workers; they were commonly known as Tinkers due to their occupation as tinsmiths. The term 'tinker' is considered pejorative today and is not used. Others were horse dealers and peddlers. However, in the last sixty to seventy years all these trades and occupations have disappeared, plastics have replaced the traditional tin buckets and bowls in the kitchen and modern transportation negates the need for both horses and peddlers.

The language of the Irish Travellers is known by a number of different names; academics tend to call it Shelta, while the Travellers use the terms Gammon or 'The Cant'. The existence of the language amongst American 'Irish Travellers' who fled the Famine is one of the chief pieces of evidence that Irish Travellers predated the Famine. Their language, nomadism, history and shared identity set them apart from settled people, whom they call buffers, in the rest of Irish society.

Irish Traveller families can be found living on Traveller sites, roadside encampments or in housing and, if mobile, are still likely to settle for a while during the winter months.

The census of 2002 reported 22,435 Travellers living in Ireland. No census data was collected in the UK, but it is estimated that a further 15,000 Irish Travellers live in Britain. British law recognises Irish Travellers as an ethnic group but, ironically, Irish law does not. In Ireland the Travellers are known as a social group. The Irish census does give us some very useful information. It shows that 63% of the population are under the age of twenty-five, while only 3.3% are over the age of sixty-five. This indicates a young and growing population and also supports the outcomes of research into the health of Travellers which demonstrates that poor access to healthcare leads to early mortality.

Useful websites
http://www.travellerheritage.ie/asp/default. asp?p=32

http://www.irishtraveller.org.uk/

Showmen or Fairground Travellers

Many of the fairs held in Britain today can trace their ancestry back to the medieval period Charters, and privileges granted then survive into the twenty-first century. The original fairs were a mark of civilisation, an opportunity to trade and participate in fun and festivities. The fairs were often an opportunity to hire labour and sometimes, as in Barnstaple in mid-September, labourers were hired until the date of the Fair when they would come along to the Fair to seek a new master.

As time has passed, transportation has improved and opportunities to trade have become much more frequent; even cattle and livestock markets have become regular events. The Fairs have changed in response to this and the Showmen have responded to the changes by creating exciting fun-filled events to take the place of the traditional Fairs.

Travelling Showpeople are thought to number around 21,000 – 25,000 and, like other traditional Travellers, they have their own language and culture. They also tend to marry within the extended group. They are commercial nomads who move from town to town during the fair season that mainly runs from February until November, with some families attending the Christmas Fairs.

The larger Fairs, such as Nottingham Goose Fair, Newcastle Town Moor, Hull Fair, Barnstaple Fair, the Cheshire Show and Stratford Fair, provide important opportunities for families to meet up during the travelling season and to socialise with old friends.

The Showman's Guild of Great Britain both governs and represents the showmen and has about 5,000 members. Most Fairs are run under the auspices of the Guild which provides unity and negotiating strength to its members. The education of the children is of concern to the Guild, and each section has an Education Liaison Officer elected from the membership.

Useful websites
For those wishing to research the history of local fairs, this gazetteer documents Fairs until the year 1516: http://www.history.ac.uk/cmh/gaz/gazweb2.html

Showmen talk about their language: http://www.bbc. co.uk/voices/recordings/group/wales-talbotgreen. shtml

Circus
Like Fairgrounds, the Circus has a long history. The Ancient Roman Circus was a building for chariot-racing, jugglers, acrobats, displays featuring trained animals and staged battles. After the fall of Rome the circus died out, with just a few travelling showmen taking their animals round to the fairs and major events of the day. The modern circus can be traced back to Philip Astley who from 9th January 1768 organised a performance of horsemanship in a ring at his riding school near Westminster Bridge in London. He soon realised that the performances were much more lucrative than his riding school and gradually added acrobats, rope dancers and jugglers to his performances. In 1782 he opened Paris' first circus and gradually rivals started to set up in competition. During the nineteenth century circuses started touring using small tents, but by the end of the century tent technology had developed and the age of the "Big Top" arrived.

The heyday of the traditional circus continued into the twentieth century, although its popularity began to decline in the 1970s when people increasingly started to question the use of animals in the circus. Other forms of popular entertainment led to increased competition.

Today Circus draws on a multi-national pool of performers, and international circuses regularly tour in Britain.

The children who travel with the circuses have difficulty accessing continuous education due to their peripatetic way of life, but they face few of the problems of accommodation, prejudice and discrimination that are faced by other Traveller pupils.

New Travellers

The New Traveller community is a mixed multi-ethnic and mixed class community that emerged from the free festivals of the 1960s. The lifestyles are quite varied, with many groups espousing a low-impact, eco-friendly lifestyle. Festivals are still a key part of the lifestyle of New Travellers and a key part of their economic survival.

A trend of travel to Europe commenced during the 1990s due to the impact of the Criminal Justice and Public Order Act, and this continues today. While it is difficult to generalise about New Travellers, it does seem that many prefer to locate in rural locations rather than urban, with Wales and south west England being particularly popular locations. This is in direct contrast to the traditional Travellers who seem to find more opportunities for work in urban areas. However, London is home to a large number of sites in places such as disused factories or warehouse yards. Few New Travellers are to be found living on local authority sites reserved for Gypsies and Travellers, and many live on unauthorised encampments in the countryside. New Travellers are known to live in barges on rivers and canals but are not usually involved in the traditional trading activities that are still common among bargees in Continental Europe.

Many New Travellers home-educate their children. This has the advantage of continuity for mobile children and enables parents to adopt an educational philosophy in keeping with their lifestyle and beliefs.

Useful websites

New Travellers – the story as seen by Alan Lodge;
http://tash.gn.apc.org/trav_fft.htm

The cultures of Gypsy Roma Traveller communities

If teachers are to provide a curriculum that affirms the culture of Gypsy Roma Traveller pupils, they will need some sense of what that culture is. In this section we will try to suggest some key components of the cultures, but it must be understood that culture is mediated through the different Gypsy Roma Traveller communities, through extended family values, and through the values of the children and their families. A family's relationship to its culture may change when it moves from quite intense communal conditions on sites to an isolated situation in housing.

If culture is alive, it needs to develop, taking account of changing circumstances. Gypsy Roma Traveller cultures have changed to take account of the arrival of motor vehicles, waggons and caravans, televisions, mobile phones and computers. Trades change over time and in different circumstances; families on official sites may develop established businesses that would not have been possible while they lived on the roadside.

It is important to understand that culture is not necessarily good or bad. Facets of culture may be regarded as good or bad depending on their context. A commitment to extended family can be seen as laudable when it comes to the care of the elderly and those with disabilities, but it may become less appropriate when a family in housing has a large number of visitors. Gypsy Roma Traveller communities tended to have larger families when infant mortality rates were high, and the older generation looked to their children to support them in old age; now, most families have more security, and the costs of raising children are increasing, smaller families are becoming more usual and culturally acceptable.

Cultures change because some people test the boundaries, and these people may attract criticism, especially if their experiments fail. There are mixed heritage relationships between Gypsy Roma Traveller groups and between Gypsy Roma Traveller community members and settled communities, which result in the merging of cultural values and, potentially, some tensions. Such families tend not to be fully accepted by either of the communities from which they derive. Some Gypsy Roma Traveller families, especially those in housing, may underplay their culture and identity in order to pass as settled people and avoid the prejudice that they might otherwise encounter; children growing up in such families may struggle to establish their sense of identity.

We all, especially young people, have multiple identities and our individual culture is likely to be an amalgamation of elements of all those identities. In school young people become aware of a range of cultures and have opportunities to develop their interests, skills and identities in ways which take them beyond the culture of their families. Parents can see this as giving them opportunities they didn't have, but they may also fear that it will take them away from their roots. When Freddy Eastwood emerged as a professional footballer, he asserted his pride in his Gypsy heritage, his pleasure that his family had been granted planning permission for their private site and his delight at knocking Manchester United out of the Carling cup.

When cultures are under threat, they tend to become more conservative and communities make a stand in defence of certain cultural principles. Ayelet Shachar calls this "reactive culturalism" and defines it as "... a strict adherence to the group's traditional laws, norms and practices as part of an identity group's resistance to external forces of change, such as secularism or modernity."[3] Some Gypsy Roma Traveller families are concerned about what their children will learn in school, both within the formal curriculum and from other pupils, to the extent that they use a range of strategies to disengage from the education system.

What are the key elements of Gypsy Roma Traveller cultures?

At the core is a relationship to nomadism. This was best summed up for us in Jason Webster's book *Duende: A journey in search of Flamenco*. Webster joined a Roma Flamenco group who had a regular booking in Madrid. One of their number enjoyed the thrill of joyriding and cocaine and was eventually killed in an accident. The response of the band was to turn its back on the stable and lucrative employment and head for Barcelona, where other members of their extended family would be able to give them a way into the music scene there. Here were Roma, who did not have a nomadic way of

[3] Shachar, A. (2001) Multicultural Jurisdictions: Cultural Differences and Women's Rights. Cambridge p35

life, responding to tragedy by moving away, using the extended family network to create opportunities.

All Gypsy Roma Traveller communities belong to those communities rather than to a particular nation or even a locality. Moving is always an option and an opportunity. Bruce Chatwin suggested in *Songlines* that there is something nomadic in all of us, and the feeling of leaving your troubles behind is one with which most of us can empathise. Ironically, many of the least mobile Travellers are those who live on permanent official sites; but they would say that if things got too bad, they would just have to move.

Eviction and enforced mobility are not part of the culture; families living on unauthorised camps are usually evicted long before they would choose to leave. But being free to move, and not feeling tied to one locality lies at the core of the culture.

The lack of identification with place and nation has been one of the reasons for the increased persecution of Roma in the post-Communist states of Eastern Europe. This lack is offensive to the nationalist leanings of the new governments and some of their right-wing citizens. Not only do Roma have their own language, but frequently Roma communities traverse national boundaries; the commitment to their own culture and identity and their failure to adopt a national identity are frequently used as justification for the prejudice and hostility they suffer.

The Roma poet Spatzo (Vittorio Mayer Pasquale) wrote the following poem, translated from Estrekarja Sinti, which eloquently illustrates key elements of Roma culture.

Freedom

We Gypsies have only one religion: freedom.
In exchange for this we renounce riches, power,
science, and glory.
We live each day as if it were the last.
When one dies, one loses all: a miserable caravan just
as a great empire.
And we believe that in that moment it is much better to
have been a Gypsy than a king.
We don't think about death. We don't fear it; here is all.
Our secret is to enjoy every day the little things
that life offers and that other men don't know how to
appreciate:
A sunny morning, a bath in the spring,
the glance of someone who loves us.
It is hard to understand these things, I know. One is
born a Gypsy.
It pleases us to walk under the stars.
They tell strange things about Gypsies
They say they read the future in the stars
and that they possess love potions.
Most people don't believe in things they can't explain
We instead don't try to explain the things we believe in.
Ours is a simple, primitive life.

It is enough for us to have the sky as a roof,
a fire to warm us,
and our songs, when we are sad.

Associated with this attachment to freedom is a reluctance to be institutionalised. It is important to recognise the extent to which schools are institutions and education requires that pupils become institutionalised. Families have said they believe their children will become soft in school, no longer resourceful and resilient, but dependent on institutions to make a living. Sometimes schools are more tolerant of pupils who are 'wild' (conforming to a stereotype) than those who are closer to the expectations of the school; it seems that when they indicate that they are prepared to be institutionalised, schools no longer feel obliged to recognise their identity and expect conformity.

The commitment to family across several generations is another key element of culture. It is virtually unheard of for members of Gypsy Roma Traveller communities to choose not to have a family or to fail to take responsibility for the old and the infirm. Schools may be frustrated when families leave with little or no notice to care for a relative, but their behaviour is entirely consistent with their commitment to family and their lack of commitment to a particular locality. Commitment to education is not grounded in the culture (in contrast to many other ethnic minority cultures) and may suffer as a consequence.

Associated with their commitment to family is an opposition to premarital relationships. Roma, Gypsies and Travellers of Irish Heritage all share this view, and various other aspects of the culture follow from it. Girls would not 'go out' with boys unless they were engaged to be married and consequently teenage marriage is regarded as quite usual. If a young couple runs away together, their families will usually sanction the relationship, whether or not they approved previously. Most Roma don't marry in church but their marriage is recognised within the community; in some cases Roma weddings have taken place below the age at which a legal marriage would be permitted. Gypsies and Irish Travellers do marry in church, and the weddings are significant community events where the culture is reinforced.

Irish Travellers are usually practising Catholics, and many Gypsies have a Pentecostal faith, which underpin their cultural values. Roma are more likely to practise the faith of the region where they have come from, including Orthodox, Roman Catholic and Muslim.

The cultures would expect a couple to start a family shortly after marrying. Roma girls will usually live with their partner's family who will help them bring up their first child. Gypsies and Irish Travellers have a similar system where, if possible, extended family members live side by side on the same site and provide support to the new mother.

In general most Gypsy Roma Traveller parents do not want their children to receive sex education, because they believe it will encourage their children to engage in premarital sexual relations. They are also unhappy about girls changing together, particularly after puberty. They feel that birth control and family planning have no place in their children's preparation for family life. Gypsy Roma Traveller families tend to be larger than average, although in recent years they have moved closer to the mean. Irish Travellers adhere to Catholic doctrine on divorce, and Gypsies discourage divorce and sex education.

Roma, who are not usually legally married, may change partners, often bringing together children from both relationships into a new family group.

Male and female roles tend to be separated, although there can be significant differences within family groups. Raising a family and taking responsibility for its education tends to be the role of women, whereas the man is more likely to be the breadwinner. In the past Gypsies and Irish Traveller women would also have worked, hawking goods from door to door and collecting scrap metal; some women regard it as progress that they are now able to stay at home and focus on their family. Because the culture gives such high value to raising a family, the child-rearing role is not seen as lower status than that of the bread-winner. The men's business tends to be a family (or extended family business) so the notion of a man pursuing his career, while the woman is tied to the home, rarely applies. The role division becomes more oppressive when families live as nuclear families separated from their extended family. Under these conditions, the contrast between the relative freedom of men to go about their business and women, tied to the home, becomes more marked.

The cultures value entrepreneurship, with most young people wanting to run their own business, probably in a field where other extended family members have experience and expertise. It is assumed that the skill required will be acquired within the community rather than in mainstream education. There is no sharp distinction between childhood and adulthood, and most young people consider themselves to be adult from their early teens. In general they are spoken to as adults and encouraged to take responsibility as they grow older. These family apprenticeships are gender-specific, girls learning to care for the home and the family, boys going out working with their fathers.

Most Gypsies and Irish Travellers have an attachment to horses, dogs and finches, understandable in terms of their history and heritage. Gypsies played their parts in both wars, caring for horses in cavalry regiments. Many Travellers keep horses. The horse fairs at Appleby, Stow and Balinasloe draw Gypsies and Irish Travellers to show their animals, compete in trotting races and trade with each other and local farmers. Roma also have a feeling for horses, even though they have been settled

for much longer. In explaining the difference between two Roma groups I was told that a distinguishing feature of the Kalderash is 'They are indifferent to horses'. True or not, it was seen as a relevant criterion. Roma dance steps replicate the pawing movements characteristic of horses.

As traders, Gypsy Roma Travellers are bound by their culture to keep to agreements made. 'My word is my bond' and a deal struck through spit and a handshake, are sufficient. It flies in the face of the allegations of dishonesty and untrustworthiness, frequently directed at these groups, that an agreement needs no signature or legal agreement. It is, however, a traditional way of doing business, appropriate to communities who are reluctant to resort to law, and who trust the written word less than physical and eye contact.

This system can work well where families are on sites, among their extended family and with trades which are in demand. Where families are isolated in housing, where men have no work or only casual work, or when family relationships break down, this system can leave young people taking too much responsibility or drifting into unemployment and crime.

Roma in Eastern Europe were less nomadic than those who migrated west, and were incorporated into feudal society as serf and slaves. Under Communism, they were included as workers and were entitled to accommodation, health care, education and employment. They experienced prejudice, in that they were often educated in special schools for the mentally retarded and channelled into unskilled labour in heavy industry, but their culture does not make the same distinction between employment and self-employment; Roma parents, most of whom are educated to secondary level, are more likely to expect schools to equip their children for employment. Gypsies and Irish Travellers tend to think that anyone who takes on permanent employment is moving away from the culture. However, some young people do take employment in supermarkets or fast food outlets, before they start a family; it would seem that the culture isn't so hostile to employment, which has developed with a focus on self-employment, because of prejudice within the labour market to these communities.

Gypsies and Irish Travellers value the opportunities horse fairs give them to meet other community members, trade, make relationships and display their wealth. The Roma also have key festivals such as that at Saintes-Marie-de-la-Mer in the Camargue.

All the Gypsy Roma Traveller communities prefer to resolve disputes without reference to the police or other outside authorities. Roma use a committee of elders called a Cris to resolve disputes; different Roma communities have their own versions of the Cris, whose decisions are more or less binding. As with the case of self-employment, the reason Gypsies and Irish Travellers do not resort to the law may relate to both their nomadic tradition (where law related to land and locality) and to their experience of prejudice at the hands of the police.

Above all, the Gypsy Roma Traveller communities are survivors. They have experienced genocide and slavery, enforced settlement and relocation, sterilisation and starvation. Their way of life has been threatened by social and economic change, by missionaries and teachers, by politicians and officials. Sometimes, when families are housed, keeping a low profile, trying to merge into the settled communities, it seems the culture may be absorbed, but then it reasserts itself, subversively or with pride. Nothing is to be gained by seeking to ignore, suppress or confront the culture; such actions will elicit defensive, aggressive or evasive responses. But recognising, respecting and valuing the culture, as is happening currently around Gypsy Roma Traveller History Month, provides the foundations for opportunities.

Pause for thought

We don't have to know the details of a culture to respect it. All children will have their own sense of identity and their culture will be a contributory part of it. How important a part and how open they want to be about it will vary. Our role as educationalists is to provide an environment where they feel able to express their identity and develop it. Betty B. Youngs[4] suggests six key elements necessary to promote self-esteem and motivation of any child.

- Physical safety (no-one will harm me)

- Emotional safety (no-one will abuse me)

- Identity (I can be proud of who I am)

- Affiliation (I belong here)

- Competence (The skills I have are recognised)

- Mission (I know what I'm doing and why).

Good classroom practice, which takes account of these elements, will also flexibly and effectively take account of culture.

- Use the families in your schools as a resource to help build a sense of what their culture is and incorporate it, subtly, into practice. Cultures are constantly changing, and different communities and families have their own interpretations and priorities. There will also be differences between generations within a family and between siblings. Our response needs to be open and flexible, a discussion not a directive.

- Gypsy Roma Traveller History Month gives us an opportunity to recognise the place of these communities in our society and schools. The focus on history allows us to present some generalisations (as we have done above) without defining how people should live now. Although Gypsy Roma Traveller History Month should affirm the status and identity of Gypsy Roma Traveller pupils in school, its primary purpose is to establish the place of Gypsy Roma Traveller communities within society as a whole. The Month is of potentially greater importance in the schools with no identified Gypsy Roma Traveller pupils and who do not reflect on their history from one year to the next, than it is in those schools who engage with Gypsy Roma Traveller communities on a daily basis.

[4] Betty B.Youngs in Dryden, G and Vos J. (2001) The Learning Revolution Network Educational Press.

Racism

"A boy said he burned Travellers' trailers up. He said if your sister was here I'd burn her up too."

Leanne, 14 years[5]

Sir Trevor Phillips (as Chair of the Commission for Race Equality) described racism towards these communities as 'the last acceptable form of racism', in that there seems to be little or no social stigma attached to expressing such racist attitudes. He drew on a survey[6] of 1,700 adults throughout England showing the extent of prejudice against minority groups in England. There were four minority groups against whom respondents most frequently expressed prejudice. These were refugees and asylum seekers, Travellers and Gypsies, people from minority ethnic communities and gay or lesbian people.

Although, most interviewees had no personal contact with Travellers and Gypsies, these groups (along with Asylum seekers) were found to be the subject of aggressive prejudice - open and explicit animosity, often backed with the threat of violence. Prejudices towards Travellers and Gypsies were expressed in economic terms. They did not appear to conform to the system by paying taxes, had a reputation for unreliable business practices and did not respect private property and cultural terms. They did not belong to a community and allegedly had a negative impact on the environment. A clear distinction was also made between Romani Gypsies, respected for their history and culture, and Travellers or modern Gypsies.

People who express prejudice against minority groups

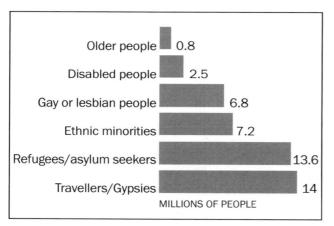

	MILLIONS OF PEOPLE
Older people	0.8
Disabled people	2.5
Gay or lesbian people	6.8
Ethnic minorities	7.2
Refugees/asylum seekers	13.6
Travellers/Gypsies	14

[5] Children's Voices: changing futures.   Research Summary. Ormiston Children's Trust

[6] Profiles of Prejudice. The nature of prejudice in England: in-depth analysis of findings (Stonewall/MORI, n.d. [2003]. Preface by Sir Herman Ouseley.)

[7] Cited on the BBC website 17th October 2004.

The press in general and the red-tops in particular delight in Gypsy (usually with a small 'G' and often with an 'i') scare stories and campaigns, such as the Sun's 'Meet your new neighbours' with an out-of-date photo of an unauthorised camp and an encouragement to join the 'Stamp on the camps campaign'. Such copy is useful in the run-up to elections because playing the anti-Traveller race card is seen as a risk-free strategy. The Daily Express ran a story, which many felt to be inflammatory, about land being compulsorily purchased to provide Gypsy sites in response to the Government's decision to set targets for site provision. We still see 'No travellers' signs, or crudely coded equivalents, outside pubs, although the test case outlawing them took place in 1989. Petrol bombs are tossed into sites, and children and their parents are attacked on their way to and from school. Newspaper headlines, in the main, characterise Traveller Communities as dirty, thieving, scrounging, anti-social strangers in our otherwise well-ordered communities. The lack of positive information and lack of capacity to celebrate the strengths and achievements of Traveller communities have resulted in high levels of prejudice and discrimination. This led Sir Trevor Phillips, then of the CRE, to remark that for Travellers 'Great Britain is still like the American Deep South (was) for black people in the 1950s'.[7]

In addition to overt personal racism, there is the more sinister institutional racism which can be found in many sectors of the economy. Clearly educational disadvantage limits the employment opportunities available to Gypsy Roma Traveller school leavers, but those who have skills and qualifications report experiences of discrimination if their identity is known. Not only did a hairdresser cancel a work experience placement when he realised that the applicant was an Irish Traveller, but the school was also criticised for not pointing this out to them when the placement was set up. For this reason many Gypsy Roma Travellers conceal their identity and families on official sites argue for their homes to have normal street addresses.

> **As well as negative media reports and being ostracised, the issue of attitudes to gypsies was raised during a controversial bonfire night celebration in 2003.**
>
> **A caravan bearing effigies of a Gypsy family and the number plate P1 KEY was burnt in Firle, East Sussex.**
>
> **This led to 12 members of a bonfire society being arrested and accused of inciting racial hatred. However, the Crown Prosecution Service (CPS) ruled they would not be prosecuted because of insufficient evidence.**
>
> **The bonfire society insisted there was no racist intent behind its actions.**

A tradition of self-employment remains a strong element in the culture of Gypsies and Irish Travellers, either providing services like landscape gardening or paving, or trading horses or used cars. Nowadays traders might use car boot sales, where who you are is irrelevant; all that matters is the quality of what you are selling and the price. No self-respecting purchaser would miss a bargain because they hold racist feelings towards any vendor. In contrast, in a conventional organisation, the prejudices of a line manger, and the hostile comments of colleagues, can make every day a nightmare and blight a career.

Over the past fifty years numerous laws have restricted the ability of Gypsy Roma Traveller communities to follow nomadic ways of living without providing viable alternatives. The Caravan Sites Act 1968 obliged local councils to make provision for Gypsies (defined as people of nomadic habit) residing in or resorting to their areas. Many councils did nothing, while others understated their Traveller populations and provided sites in locations which would never have been considered suitable for residential accommodation. When families bought land and tried to develop their own sites, they were frequently thwarted by planning laws. They found themselves in a Catch 22 situation; apply for planning permission before you move on and it will be refused; move on and apply for retrospective permission and you will be pilloried in the local press for trying to get round the law.

The term 'pikey', a contraction of people who live on turnpikes, has been a term of abuse for Gypsies for generations. The term has become current again to describe people who we look down upon, often because they lack style and class.

Why does racism persist with Gypsy Roma Travellers?

Any nomadic group is likely to suffer from prejudice directed at those who don't belong. To some extent this might be mitigated by the services that nomads offer, whether it be pot-repairing, horse-dealing or musicianship; but as society has developed into one in which the demand for nomadic skills is obviated by transport networks and disposable commodities, unmitigated prejudice remains. The prejudices are often the worst case scenarios; any site will be associated with the conditions prevailing on unregulated unauthorised camps.

But the prejudice remains, and may even become worse when families cease to be nomadic. Families living in housing frequently have to move because they become the focus of racist attacks from their neighbours. The Roma in Eastern Europe have been settled for generations, but are still the focus of widespread and overt prejudice. Roma were enslaved for four centuries in what is now Romania and more than a million died in the Holocaust.

In the UK the population of Gypsy Roma Travellers is thought to be between 200,000 and 300,000 – 0.5% of the population. Unlike other similar size minorities (Jews and Bangladeshis) they are distributed around the whole country, and many try to pass as settled people. In practice they represent a small minority in virtually every area.

Inter-racial understanding and respect usually develop through social contact and community organisation. Children attending ethnically diverse schools, colleagues in equal opportunities work settings, corner shop owners and cab drivers, bring most of the population into contact with the main minority groups in situations where it becomes increasingly difficult to maintain an attitude of prejudice. The historic lack of engagement with education, and the ongoing exclusion of Gypsy Roma Travellers from most work settings, the small size of the communities and their reticence about asserting their identity prevent prejudice against Gypsy Roma Traveller communities dissipating.

Gypsy Roma Traveller sense of community derives from their ethnicity, not from the locality where they live. It derives from community events (weddings, funerals, horse fairs, festivals) rather than the place where they live. As such they tend to remain as outsiders and are viewed with suspicion by the people who feel they have an interest in the locality. Roma groups in Eastern Europe cross national boundaries and one of the tensions between them and other residents of post-communist states is their failure to embrace nationalism and national languages. Parallels exist between Gypsy Roma Travellers and other communities with nomadic heritages (including first Americans and indigenous Australians). The prejudice such communities suffer relates to cultural values and perceptions, and is more persistent than that suffered by newly-arrived migrant or refugee communities who find ways of accommodating to the dominant culture.

Refugee and migrant groups tend to include a mix of social classes. It is easier for skilled professionals and business people to prove that they are not economic migrants, and they are more likely to have the wherewithal to cover the costs of relocation. In contrast, educationally disadvantaged and socially excluded minorities have relatively few community members with the vision and confidence to take on community leadership roles. Roma, because they were less nomadic and were socially more included under Communism, have more robust community organisations.

Finally, most minority communities have a degree of self-organisation which enables them to support each other, promote their identity and culture and confront racism and prejudice. Although there are Gypsy Roma Traveller organisations, they tend not to be very broad-based and rely on the support on gorgios, gadje or buffers (the names used by Gypsies, Roma and Travellers of Irish Heritage for people who do not belong to their ethnic group).

Pause for thought

• Develop a culture of mutual respect within school so all children feel safe and confident to feel proud of their identity.

• Make special efforts to ensure all parents have the opportunity to be involved in the life of the school.

• Even if prevailing values in the locality outside the school are hostile to Gypsy Roma Travellers, the school can provide a haven.

• Don't be confused by skin colour; victims of racism can be racist too. A Gypsy can be racist to a Somali child or an Irish Traveller Child and vice versa. Schools need strategies to deal with inter-racial tensions as well as white-on-black racism.

Community Cohesion

From September 2007 schools have been under a new duty to promote community cohesion. This duty springs, at least in part, from the Equality Act of 2006 which established the Commission for Equality and Human Rights. This legislation brought together the monitoring of the:

• Sex Discrimination Act 1975

• Race Relations Act 1976 as amended in 2000

• Disability Discrimination Act 1995 as amended in 2005

• Human Rights Act 1998

• Equal Pay Act

• Equality Act (Sexual Orientation) Regulations

• Equality Act (Gender realignment) Regulations

• Special Needs and Disability Act

• Employment Equality (Religion or Belief) regulations 2003

The outcome for schools was the Education and Inspections Act 2006 (Duty to Promote Community Cohesion). The Duty to Promote Community Cohesion requires the school to have policies to promote equality, which can take the form of either a 'single equality policy' or a number of individual policies which cover each of the areas of Race, Gender, Sexual Orientation, Disability, Religion and Belief, employment and Human Rights.

What is Community Cohesion?

Alan Johnson, Secretary of State for Education and Skills, speaking in Parliament on 2nd November 2006, defined Community Cohesion as follows:

"By community cohesion, we mean working towards a society in which there is a common vision and sense of belonging by all communities; a society in which the diversity of people's backgrounds and circumstances is appreciated and valued; a society in which similar life opportunities are available to all; and a society in which strong and positive relationships exist and continue to be developed in the workplace, in schools and in the wider community". [8]

What are the implications for schools with regard to Gypsy Roma Traveller pupils?

In schools that promote community cohesion to include Gypsy Roma Traveller communities we would expect to see the following responses to the duty:

Teaching, learning and curriculum

• The curriculum takes into account the range of communities that exist in Britain and in the wider world. All schools, including those with no identified Gypsy Roma Travellers on roll, should find opportunities within the curriculum to affirm the place of these communities within a wider society. Jake Bowers, a Romani journalist, described the impact of the invisibility of these communities in a special issue of Traveller Times published to celebrate the first Gypsy Roma Traveller History Month in 2008.

"Go to most museums, libraries and schools and nothing about our history and culture is kept or taught. The result is a widespread ignorance about who we are, which sometimes turns to hatred, fear and misunderstanding. In schools, children learn more about the Romans, Vikings or even fairies than they do about our cultures and what we have contributed to this world." [9]

• Schools develop strategies which enable Gypsy Roma Traveller pupils to achieve in school and reach significantly higher levels of attainment than at present, through catch-up programmes, personalisation and the provision of Distance Learning.

• Teaching methods and styles take into account the life experiences and learning styles of all minority ethnic pupils including Gypsy Roma Traveller pupils.

[8] Based on the Government and the Local Government Association's definition first published in Guidance on Community Cohesion, LGA, 2002 and resulting from the Cantle Report in 2001.

[9] Jake Bowers, Romani Journalist. See the whole article on: *http://www.grthm.co.uk/whatis.php*

- Books, displays and resources in all schools reflect the diversity of British communities. All schools will be able to get advice on ways of including Traveller perspectives within their curriculum from Traveller Education Support Services.

Equity and excellence

- The schools admission process is fair and equitable to all, including mid-term arrivals and short-stay Gypsy Roma Travellers.

- Monitoring the progress of Minority Ethnic and Traveller Children is the responsibility of a named member of staff and a governor, and should include Gypsy Roma Traveller pupils who are on roll at the school, whether or not they have ascribed to the Gypsy Roma Traveller or Irish Heritage categories.

- SLT and Governors ensure that sufficient time is allocated for regular staff training on target setting for vulnerable groups aimed at narrowing the attainment gaps.

- The school provides additional support and guidance to parents and students who may be unfamiliar with the options available at Key Stages 4 and 5.

- When schools monitor attendance by gender, ethnicity and disability it is important that Traveller Attendance is correctly recorded to distinguish between periods of travelling and casual absence and respond appropriately (see chapter on Attendance).

- The schools systems for disciplining and rewarding pupils are applied equally to all pupils, taking into account cultural differences between different groups.

- All pupils should be able to access the full range of teaching groups and this is monitored by gender, ethnicity, EAL, SEN and disability. All pupils access 14-19 opportunities and Traveller pupils are not denied access to some courses because they travel for part of the year.

- The school monitors exclusions by, among others, ethnicity including Gypsy Roma Travellers.

Engagement and extended services

- Schools work collaboratively with other agencies to provide extended services including education, resources and training to all their communities, developing, for example, 'Key skills', Citizenship and ESOL.

- Schools develop partnerships with all parents, including those from under-represented or hard-to-reach groups, and monitor their success in achieving this objective.

- Communication with home takes account of the home language and literacy levels of all families.

- Social events are arranged to include all parents and the school encourages participation by parents and families who might otherwise feel marginalised.

Identity and Ascription

There are two ethnic categories that identify Gypsy Roma Traveller children - Gypsy/Roma (WROM) and Traveller of Irish Heritage (WIRT). Many families choose the equally accurate, but less contentious, WBRI (White British), WIRI (White Irish), WEEU (White East European), WEUR (White European) or WOTW (White other).

This is a recognised national issue with fewer pupils ascribed to the two categories than Gypsy, Roma and Irish Traveller pupils known to Traveller Education Support Services. It is estimated that as few as half of Gypsies, Roma and Irish Travellers ascribe to the categories. Figures from six London boroughs suggest that Irish Travellers have higher rates of ascription than Gypsies and Roma.

There may be other Gypsy Roma Travellers who are not known to the TESS and who have not identified themselves. In addition there are other Traveller groups who do not fall into either of those categories; New Travellers, Circus and Fairground families, for example, or families who live on waterways and families of mixed heritage.

In March 2009 the DCSF introduced a non-mandatory change in the way schools collect ethnicity data requested from parents involving the categories of 'Gypsy/Roma' and 'Traveller of Irish heritage'. They recommended that from autumn 2009 there should be three separate categories: Gypsy, Roma and Traveller. The rationale given is that Travellers who are not of Irish heritage (eg. Scottish, Welsh or English Travellers) are discouraged from identifying themselves. It does not appear to be intended as an encouragement to New Travellers or circus and fairground families to identify although this may be the outcome. The reason given for separation of the Gypsy/Roma group is the belief that some Roma families are put off identifying by the pejorative connotations of the word "Gypsy". This proposal involves no change to the way schools or LAs hold or report their data as they will aggregate the numbers into the existing two categories of 'Gypsy/Roma' and 'Traveller of Irish heritage'. Most Gypsy Roma Traveller parents anticipate that if their children's identity is known, they will be subject to some form of discrimination, racial bullying or abuse. With 35% of the population admitting to holding racist attitudes to Gypsies and Travellers[10], it would be surprising if such attitudes did not permeate the staff and children of schools. The benefits of identification lie in general improvements to the education system; the direct benefits to individuals may be outweighed by the disadvantages of being "out" as target for racism.

There is a cultural tradition of "passing" as settled people, gorgios, gadje, buffers. Jake Bowers eloquently describes the choice he made as a Gypsy parent when he enrolled his daughter in Nursery school.

"There's not a child that hasn't wondered what it is like to be invisible, but most Gypsy and Traveller kids can tell you exactly what a cloak of secrecy feels like. It allows you to keep your head down and pass by unnoticed. It's something we are taught as children and practise as adults. Hiding comes as second nature to a people that have been chased and persecuted for 500 years. "Pukker nixies" (say

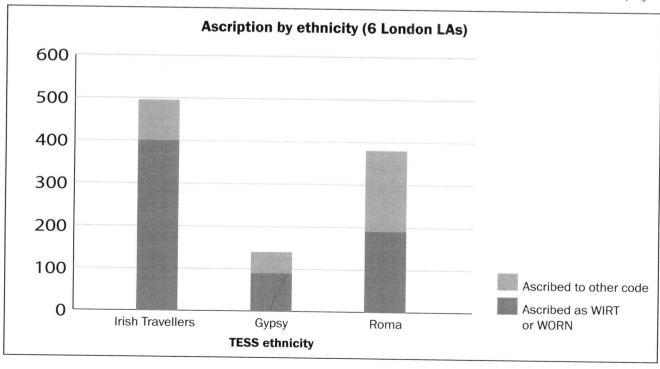

Ascription by ethnicity (6 London LAs)

TESS ethnicity — Irish Travellers, Gypsy, Roma

Legend: Ascribed to other code; Ascribed as WIRT or WORN

nothing) the old ones said in Romany, and I was about to follow their advice.

But then I remembered the countless Gypsy kids I've met over the past year standing proudly by displays they've made in schools in connection with the first Gypsy, Roma and Traveller History Month. ... The elders teach you wisdom, and the young ones teach you hope, so I ticked the box and a little Gypsy girl's cloak of secrecy was hung on its hook." [11]

Families are entitled to choose whatever category they feel appropriate, but it is important that schools make parents aware of the choices available to them, and explain that the purpose of ethnic monitoring is to ensure that all children receive their full educational entitlement. The school's guidance can be particularly important where families are unfamiliar with the UK education system, have limited English or struggle with literacy.

Roma have particular reasons to be reluctant to identify themselves; they experienced identification, transportation and extermination during the Porajmos.[12] In most of Eastern Europe Roma were forcibly settled in the 1950s and still begin their education in remedial special schools without even having the chance to start at a regular school.[13] Most Roma in the UK enjoy the anonymity of their Eastern European status; the attacks of Romanian Roma in Belfast[14] by neo-Nazi Combat 18 suggest that their judgements are prudent.

In some cases families may not choose the identifiers, but can still be quite open about belonging to Gypsy Roma Traveller communities. In other cases their identity may become known when they begin to feel comfortable in the school. In such cases the school might take an opportunity to encourage such parents to review their choice of ethnic category. As with other communities, there are mixed heritage relationships resulting in a range of cultural issues that may have an impact on a child's education.

[10] See chapter on Racism

[11] Jake Bowers' Blog, Hiding to nothing Traveller Times online www.travellerstimes.org.uk

[12] Romani term introduced by Romani scholar and activist Ian Hancock to describe attempts by the regime in Nazi Germany to exterminate most of the Romani people of Europe as part of the Holocaust.

[13] European Roma Rights Center Country Reports Series (European Roma Rights Center Country Reports Series), issue: No.13 / 2003, p.38.

[14] Henry McDonald 'Romanian gypsies beware beware. Loyalist C18 are coming to beat you like a baiting bear' The Observer, Sunday 21 June 2009.

[15] Wilkin, A., Derrington C. and Foster B. (2009), Literature Review - Improving outcomes for Gypsy, Roma and Traveller pupils, DCSF.

The Race Relations Acts specifically protect Romani Gypsies and Travellers of Irish Heritage. School staffs should be aware that their school's race equality schemes include these groups and should be sensitive to potentially racist elements in bullying and abuse. For example, the word 'pikey', which is used widely among young people, was originally an abusive term for Gypsy and is offensive to most Gypsy Roma Traveller pupils. The protection of race equality policies should apply to all Gypsy Roma Traveller pupils, whether or not they have ascribed to the two categories.

The Commission for Racial Equality (now the Commission for Equalities and Human Rights) identified the racism suffered by Gypsies and Travellers as the last acceptable form of racism which, unlike that towards most other communities, showed no sign of diminishing. All schools have a responsibility to promote race equality and community cohesion. There is a number of curriculum areas - English, Media Studies, Humanities, Music, Art, PSHE and Citizenship - where the culture, history and contribution of Gypsy Roma Traveller communities can be considered in a positive and affirming way. The school Self-Evaluation Form provides schools with opportunities to record this work.

In 2008 the DCSF published "The Inclusion of Gypsy, Roma and Traveller Children and Young People" which offers strategies to persuade children, families, schools and LAs of the benefits of ascription to the WIRT and WROM codes. The table opposite summarises the benefits and the beneficiaries with respect to teaching and learning, good race relations and effective monitoring and target setting.

TESSs identify Gypsy Roma Traveller pupils through family and community links, rather than ascription; schools may also become aware over time that children who are ascribed to a different group are from Gypsy Roma Traveller heritages. In some cases, even where the TESS introduces a family to a school, they will still select an alternative ascription. Support is normally offered to schools and families on the basis of identity rather than ascription.

The first meeting between a school and a family may be crucial to establishing the relationship between them, although practice varies considerably between schools. The completion of forms may be seen as an administrative task, normally left to parents, but where they have difficulties with the language or literacy, they can be supported by office staff. Many parents will find these times quite stressful, operating outside their comfort zone in unfamiliar surroundings, not wishing to say the wrong thing. These are not conditions best suited to accuracy and openness.

The initial school meeting can be crucial to establishing a relationship of trust between the parents and the school. Gypsy Roma Traveller families tend not to be institutionalised and therefore the concept of

	Children	Parents	Schools	LA
Pride in identity	✓	✓	✓	✓
Human right to have identity recognised	✓	✓	✓	✓
Psychological, social and personal importance of identity in effective learning	✓	✓	✓	✓
Allowing racists and bullies to go unchallenged	✓	✓		
Duties under Race Relations Acts			✓	✓
Community cohesion	✓	✓		
Benefits to family and community	✓			
Identified pupils can be role models and ambassadors	✓	✓		
Strong friendships based on openness and honesty	✓	✓		
Appropriate support from teachers	✓	✓		
Self-esteem and respect		✓	✓	✓
Burden on child of living a lie		✓		
Successful learning draws on life experience		✓		
Inclusive curriculum			✓	
Relationships between school and family			✓	
Accurate ascription increases funding			✓	✓
Data collection and target setting			✓	✓
School improvement and self-evaluation			✓	✓

trusting an institution will not come naturally to them. Many studies[15] have emphasised the importance of families having a person or people within the institution with whom they can relate and develop a relationship of trust. If families are to come to trust the school as a whole, it will be as a result of an educational process starting from the admission meeting. Policies to protect children, school expectations, financial and educational support available need to be made explicit and real. Ethnic monitoring, its purpose and the benefits of identification should be included in this initial discussion.

Pause for thought

- Does the welcoming process in school encourage openness about identity?

- How much are staff involved in the interviewing process prepared to encourage openness about identity?

- Does the LA provide any guidance to schools about these issues?

- Is there provision for families changing their ascription as their relationship with the school develops?

- Is the ethnic identifier chosen on enrolment also used when monitoring exclusions and racial incidents?

- Does the ascription change on transfer to secondary school? If it does, why does it happen and what can be done about it?

Admission to school

The legal position

The Education Act 1996 places Local Education Authorities under a duty to provide education for all school-age children in their area, appropriate to their age, abilities and aptitudes and any special educational needs they may have. This duty extends to all children residing in their area, whether permanently or temporarily. It therefore includes Gypsy Roma Traveller children, regardless of the security of their accommodation or their immigration status. Gypsy and Traveller children should be admitted to schools on the same basis as any other children.

The recently revised School Admission Code is designed to make admission to school fairer and more transparent and requires that local authorities consult with the range of their communities.

Admission to schools - practical considerations

When Traveller pupils first arrive in an area, it is vital to gain a school place quickly to maintain educational continuity. This is because it demonstrates our values and commitment to the education of the children and the value we place on Traveller children's access to school. How we act from the start of our relationship with a family sets the tone for future engagement. There may be parental reluctance to allow the children to go to school and there can be many reasons for this. Some reasons might be fear of eviction, no access to the correct school uniform, negative media coverage, fear for the children's safety, difficulty with transport, and insufficient adults both to escort the children to school and also ensure that the caravans are not left unattended and subject to attack or vandalism. Local Education Welfare teams, alongside TESSs will support the school and family to address these issues, but it is important that they ensure that the children do gain speedy access to education.

The role of the Admissions team

The new School Admission Code is intended to be both fair and transparent and has led to a review of admissions procedures in many local authorities. It can seem fair to design a system for admissions that suits the majority. Highly mobile families, including newly arrived families and those without stable accommodation, are often the most vulnerable, without local knowledge and possibly with language or literacy difficulties. It is important that the admission system is fair and equitable for all children. Local authorities now have Fair Access Panels to ensure that there is equity in allocating school places. Where these comply with Equality Impact Needs Assessments they do not delay the admission of Traveller pupils.

Transport to school

Once the Admissions team has offered a school place, the next hurdle to cross is the physical one of getting the child from home to school safely. There are many different circumstances for the Transport team to consider, and differences between rural and urban settings. In fact, some urban boroughs may not have Transport teams at all as they are geographically too small to require one. In these circumstances families may face transport issues with no recourse to a Transport Department.

Many parents will have the ability to fulfil their role in getting their children to school using only family resources. For others, it can be very difficult. The TESS will attempt to address these issues with the family and the school, but a degree of flexibility and understanding of the exceptional circumstances experienced by these groups may be required.

Travellers on roadside encampments cannot leave their homes unattended for fear of vandalism and attack; someone always has to be on site to watch over their homes. Vehicles used to tow caravans double up as the means by which males earn a living, so won't be available for escorting children to and from school. Mobile Travellers are often in unfamiliar areas and do not know their way around. Because of poor access to education over many generations, there are many adults who struggle with reading road signs and maps, and the likelihood of swift eviction reduces the urgency to gain detailed local knowledge. There can be other circumstances, such as pregnancy and ill health, which demand attendance at hospital as well as everyday tasks such as shopping and doing the laundry to be undertaken. These are circumstances which demand additional consideration and raise issues that are not often faced by the local population in housing, who would have few issues about locking up their homes and leaving them unattended.

Families with several children arriving mid-term may find that their children are offered places in different schools. This may require long journeys and complex travel plans to enable parents to accompany them to each school. Although many LAs provide free travel for school age children and young people, parents accompanying children will be expected to pay full fares.

Gypsy Roma Travellers are vulnerable to racist attacks, both where they live and on journeys to school. This can be particularly true if there are tensions associated with unauthorised camps, or hostile local attitudes to refugees and economic migrants. Parents put the highest priority on safeguarding their children and, unless practical travel arrangements can be put in place, may keep their children at home and accept the consequences.

Outreach work with families

The role of Traveller Education support professionals is particularly important with families who are between schools and have often newly arrived in an area. Once families have made a positive engagement with a school, this support can be gradually withdrawn, although most TESSs remain available to both the family and the school should their advice be needed.

Almost all Gypsy Roma Traveller families need to gain access to an outreach worker at some time during their children's education. This is a key worker who can build trusting relationships, assess needs that may not be purely educational but which may impact on children's education, signpost to other services, engaging with those services to create the circumstances that will enable the children to attend school and know about practical arrangements such as school start and finish times, uniform and school meals. Parents will need to know who to contact in case of any difficulty and, due to low literacy levels, there is little point in an information brochure.

Schools

The initial meeting between the school and the parents can be crucial in laying the foundations of a relationship which will enable the child or children to get the most out of their time in the school. Safety will be high on the parents' list of priorities, because they are giving their children over to an institution outside their community and culture. They will want to know how their children will be protected and who to contact in the event of problems.

Schools will need to assess how much information parents might need, based on their knowledge and experience of the education system. Circus and fairground families, who are used to moving from school to school, may be clear what they need from the school and may want the opportunity to explain how their Distance Learning programmes operate. Parents whose own educational experience was unsatisfactory may need more reassurance that their children's experience will be different.

Asylum applicants and families arriving from other countries in the European Union may need more basic information about how the education system works in the UK. Issues such as ethnic monitoring and Special Educational Needs may be interpreted differently by parents who have arrived from countries where many Roma children are segregated in schools for the educationally retarded.

No guidance can cover every situation, so it is important to make sure parents are put at their ease, are given the time and opportunity to raise any concerns and are reassured that they and their children are welcome.

When children are admitted to school it is important that they should be made to feel welcome and follow a very practical induction programme introducing them to the school, the staff, the benefits of belonging to the community and its geography, as well as the Code of Conduct.

Academic assessment is vital to placing a pupil correctly and designing a personalised programme, but in the earliest stages this should be based on observation and formative assessment rather than formal testing. The pupil's family may be able to indicate the previous school attended and it may be possible to obtain pupil records, but this can be more difficult than one would imagine.

Often, despite teachers' convictions that children are able and should be achieving well, the children themselves haven't the self-confidence in their ability to be successful in school. This attitude has a number of causes: their mobility, the treatment of their communities in the media and by local residents during planning applications and appeals and the history of bullying and racism against Gypsy Roma Travellers, combined with the feeling that they cannot keep up with other pupils in the classroom. Building trust and careful planning for induction into school are keys to creating the warm, welcoming and purposeful environment that assists Gypsy Roma Traveller children to feel that they belong to and are participants in a school system that is as much for them as it is for all the others. Many Gypsy Roma Traveller children describe school as if they are alien intruders into a world meant for others and where schools can create an atmosphere of safety, purpose and belonging, it goes a long way towards settling children into school.

Funding for Traveller pupils admitted to schools mid-year

There is no guaranteed funding for Traveller pupils who are not attending a school on the third Thursday in January and who are not included in the Annual School Census that is taken on that date. However, some local authorities can come to shared funding arrangements for pupils who regularly attend schools in two local authority areas.

There may also be flexibility in the Dedicated Schools Grant for gaining funding for pupils falling into a local authority's classification of 'deprived' which often includes free school meals as an indicator, but sometimes also includes Ethnicity. The DCSF publication "Breaking the link between Poverty and Disadvantage", published in March 2009, has an annex which opens up the issue of FSM and disadvantage further. It is hoped that ongoing consultation may leave room for further development when this is looked at again in 2010.

Pause for Thought

- Questions for school admissions teams would be: how quickly and efficiently can you place a newly arrived pupil in school? Could your system admit a child to school on the day after an application is made? Would it take a week? A month? We would contend that effective practice in admissions should enable you to offer a school place to Travelling children and other mobile pupils in three days.

- Can schools transport make exceptions to the usual regulations for vulnerable children and can these decisions be made quickly enough to facilitate speedy access to school?

- If schools transport cannot make exceptions sufficiently and quickly, does the co-ordinator for Traveller Education Support Services have access to a budget that can provide transport in these cases?

- Does your local authority have outreach workers and communication systems that support your capacity to reach out to these communities and ensure that they are safe and have access to a range of services?

- Are schools in a position to organise an induction programme for newly-arrived Traveller pupils? If not where would they go for support in developing such a programme?

- What systems are in place to facilitate formative assessment of newly-arrived pupils?

Attendance in an Every Child Matters context

If you asked teachers who work with Gypsy Roma Traveller pupils "What single thing would improve the educational experience of this group of children?" they would respond "better attendance." We find that teachers are often willing to go the extra mile - preparing differentiated work, gathering resources from within the school - only to be frustrated when the child on whom they are focusing doesn't turn up when expected. If Gypsy Roma Traveller children are to narrow the gap between themselves and their peers, the minimum requirement is that they give their teachers a chance to engage with their learning. Negative attitudes to these communities can stem as much from frustration as prejudice or intolerance.

The chart below illustrates the uniquely high levels of absence of pupils ascribing to the Gypsy Roma and Traveller of Irish Heritage ethnic codes. The levels of absence are 3.5 and 4.3 times greater than the average for all pupils, and more than double that of the next worst attending group.

These teachers are right that absence contributes to and compounds the educational disadvantage of these communities, but too often it is seen as a failing of the child or family rather than as part of a much more complex issue relating to social exclusion and deprivation.

Enjoy and achieve

At the most superficial level, if pupils don't attend school, they cannot expect to be able to keep up with, or close the gap on, their peers. Not only will they learn less, but also their learning will be disrupted, so they won't understand what they are learning today because of what they missed yesterday. In our experience, class teachers are prepared to put in a lot of effort to make the curriculum accessible to pupils who have missed out on education, but they will not put in the time if they do not know whether the child they are trying to help will turn up. Other children are unlikely to include them in their friendship circles if they can't rely on them to be in school.

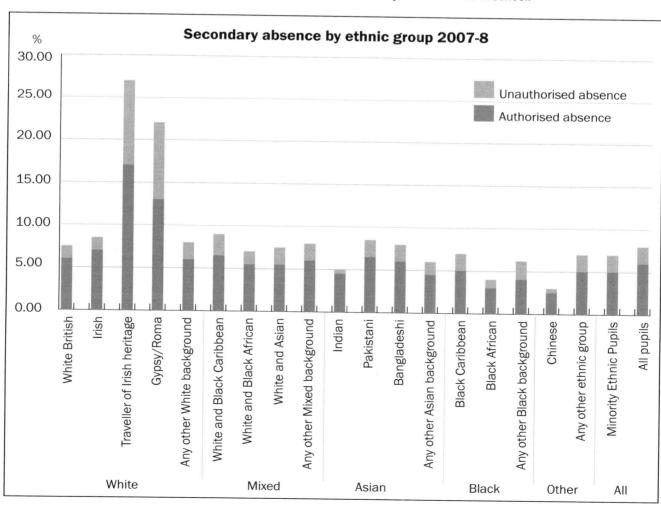

Secondary absence by ethnic group 2007-8

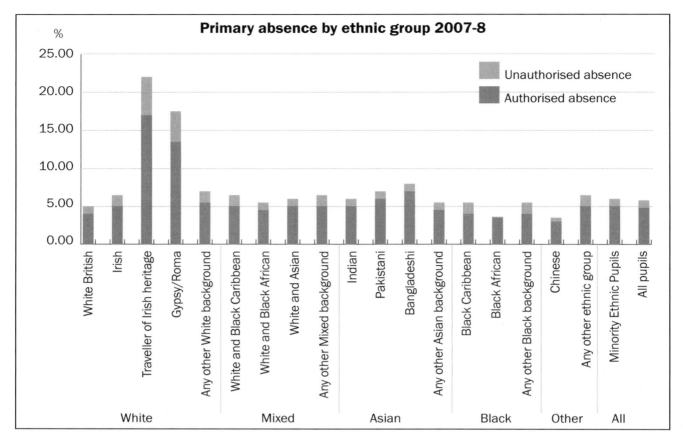

Primary absence by ethnic group 2007-8

Legend: Unauthorised absence, Authorised absence

Categories along x-axis: White British, Irish, Traveller of Irish heritage, Gypsy/Roma, Any other White background (White); White and Black Caribbean, White and Black African, White and Asian, Any other Mixed background (Mixed); Indian, Pakistani, Bangladeshi, Any other Asian background (Asian); Black Caribbean, Black African, Any other Black background (Black); Chinese, Any other ethnic group (Other); Minority Ethnic Pupils, All pupils (All)

We have a vicious circle here. If pupils don't feel included and can't understand or access the classroom activities, they'll find reasons not to attend school. But if they don't attend school, they won't encourage the school to welcome and accommodate them.

But there are other reasons why children don't attend school which relate to the ECM agenda.

Health

Gypsy Roma Traveller communities are known to suffer significantly worse health than average, including higher infant mortality rates, shorter life spans, heart and lung problems and depressive illnesses. Those who live in poor accommodation – temporary housing, sites in locations unfit for residence, unauthorised camps, overcrowded conditions – are more likely to suffer poor health. Parents with their own health issues may not be able to care properly for their children and may need them to act as carers. Adults with poor health may be dependent on benefits and poverty can be associated with poor diet and health.

Safety

Pupils who arrive mid-phase, or who do not enrol in schools at appropriate times, may find they do not get a place in the school nearest to where they live (particularly if it is a popular one) and need to travel some distance to get to one with vacancies. Where there are several children in a family, they may be placed in different schools. Children who are new to an area are unfamiliar with bus services and are reluctant to seek the help of strangers, may be at risk on the journeys to and from schools.

Where possible, parents will try and drop their children off at their different schools, but they may have difficulties picking them up after school. Parents without transport may find the costs of accompanying their children, and the uncertainties of being there to meet them, can be a source of anxiety and increase their reluctance to send them to school. The reality and the fear of racist bullying and attacks play on the minds of many Gypsy Roma Traveller parents and their children, and these concerns will impact on attendance.

Economic well-being

Although some Gypsy Roma Traveller families are comfortably off, the majority are not. More than half are eligible for free school meals. Sending your children to school can be an expensive business, especially if you have a number of children, they are growing, they go to different schools and you move from school to school. Even though schools expect good attendance, many secondary schools send pupils home if they are not in proper uniform. Not wearing proper uniform can result in detentions, and if detentions are after school, may

[16] Roma who were living in the UK as Asylum Applicants when the countries they came from joined the European Union were granted exceptional leave to remain after a Judicial Review by Mr Justice Collins and were entitled to benefits while they sought work.

[17] Edemariam, A. (2009) Unhappy return: fear and loathing await fugitives from Belfast racism Guardian Newspaper 27/6/09 on-line at http://www.guardian.co.uk/world/2009/jun/26/race-attacks-on-belfast-roma

have safety implications for the pupils travelling home alone.

Roma who have arrived from Eastern Europe since their countries joined the European Union[16] have no entitlement to benefits until they have been in registered employment for two years. As a result, these families are not eligible for free school meals or housing benefit. Most find casual work, such as cleaning under a gang master system which is unregistered and pays them below the minimum wage. Some sell the Big Issue or scavenge domestic refuse. They live in the private rented sector with several families sharing the rent. Some squat vacant properties and experience a cycle of evictions similar to families living on unauthorised camps. It is indicative of the levels of poverty in Eastern Europe that such an existence represents an improvement on conditions they have left behind.[17]

Making a contribution

Gypsy Roma Traveller communities have a strong sense of social responsibility for their community and extended family. Caring for family members who are aged or unwell is a social obligation that can interfere with school attendance. Children with serious disabilities are cared for by their families, which can put additional pressures on other children. Gypsy Travellers have higher than average incidence of health problems related to stress, anxiety, diet and lifestyle.[18] The cultural expectation that children will care for their younger siblings and that women have a primary caring role can result in Gypsy Roma Traveller children, girls in particular, taking responsibility for caring for unwell parents and keeping the family functioning. This demand becomes all the more intense where families are not in contact with local services or are suspicious of them.

Older people are rarely placed in care homes and it is normal for their children to move to care for them towards the end of their life. Funerals are significant family events and there is an expectation that family and friends of the deceased attend to pay their respects. Most Irish Travellers will be buried in family plots in Ireland and Roma funerals could be anywhere in Europe.

The myth that Gypsy Roma Traveller communities make little contribution to society as a whole stems from the perception that they are not part of wider society. If people feel socially excluded, they are unlikely to receive the benefits of belonging to broader society and they will find it more difficult to make a contribution.

The sub-culture of sites

In a recent survey[19] of site residents in London, fewer than half said they were satisfied with their accommodation. Despite their dissatisfaction, however, families on sites were likely to have lived there for more than five years; only 14% said they would consider moving into housing. The same study, also found that slightly more than half the families in housing would prefer to live on sites.

Many sites are in poor locations, badly maintained and poorly managed, but families prefer to live there because of "the sense of community" of living among their own people. When the Commission for Racial Equality first began to look for ways of promoting better race relations between settled and travelling communities, it soon came to focus on the tensions around sites and camps, and the national shortage of good quality, well-run and appropriately-located official sites.[20] The Equality and Human Rights Commission has taken over the brief and concluded:

"Providing adequate accommodation for Gypsies and Travellers is both eminently possible and an essential foundation for good community relations. Only two years away from the 2011 Government deadline, it is clear that too little progress has been made towards meeting this need."[21]

Traveller Education professionals have been allies of families fighting for decent sites, understanding how important the issue was to them, and witnessing the difficulties they faced in housing, isolated from their extended families and at odds with their neighbours. In practice, however, the correlation between school attendance and accommodation that reflects the culture can be a negative one. Secondary students regularly have to run the gauntlet of other site residents, of school age and older, who have a different view of the benefits of school.

In our view, good site design, locations and management can address these issues, although only the latter can be addressed in the short term. The sub-culture of a site will reflect its location and its size: if the site is nowhere near other accommodation, it will effectively become a ghetto, a place where no-one other than the people who live there, and possibly those who do business with them, will go. Some sites like this can become no-go areas for the people who are meant to manage them, for professionals and the

[18] Parry, G. et al (2004) The Health Status of Gypsies & Travellers in England: Summary of a report to the Department of Health 2004 The University of Sheffield, School of Health and Related Research.

[19] Fordham Research (2008) London Boroughs' Gypsy and Traveller Accommodation Needs Assessment on-line at http://mayor.london. gov.uk/mayor/housing/gtana/docs/report.pdf pp.5-6.

[20] CRE (2006) Common Ground Equality, good race relations and sites for Gypsies and Irish Travellers.

[21] Equality and Human Rights Commission (2009) Gypsies and Travellers: simple solutions for living together. ISBN 978 1 84206 098 8.

police. It has long been understood that the location and design of housing can have a significant effect on how people behave, and it is no different with sites.

Small sites, effectively occupied by a single extended family group, are for most families the ideal. Indeed, the growing numbers of small private sites are frequently developed on the same basis. Small local authority sites require less management, although describing them as self-managing is, for the local authority, to abdicate responsibility for fair allocation, health and safety, and duties of care. Smaller sites tend to be more acceptable to neighbours and can be located in residential neighbourhoods. It is more likely they will become less like ghettos, with children bringing school friends to visit. Such visits do much to break down prejudice and suspicion. If sites are on the route to school, other pupils may well pick up their friends as they go by, so education is less likely to be disrupted by family members being unwell, the car not starting or the prospect of a dreary tramp through an industrial wasteland.

Ghettos are defined as "Ethnically or racially segregated areas".
Many ghettos were established by mutual agreement and may be relatively affluent.
Studies have shown that, compared with families of the same ethnicity outside the ghetto,
- **disadvantage passes from generation to generation**
- **skills and norms influenced by peers often result in dropping out of school, unemployment and criminal behaviour**
- **attitudes to residents become based on stereotypes rather than reality**

Decisions about the location, design and management of sites are rarely taken in consultation with Children's Services, but they should be, because they can have an impact across the whole ECM agenda. Conversely, sites which become magnets for Traveller youth can become increasingly difficult to manage, and a vicious circle from which no-one benefits is generated.

Unpacking poor attendance

The figures on persistent absence make even more depressing reading than those on overall absence. Over a third of Travellers of Irish Heritage and more than a quarter of Gypsy Roma pupils are identified as persistent absentees, ten and eight times the average for all pupils, respectively.

Unfortunately, the persistent absentees will include several different groups of children whose circumstances need to be addressed in different ways. It is important to establish which category the children fall into because the response may be different in each case.

1. **Pupils who are able to attend and choose not to** are truants. They need to be followed up as a matter of urgency by school attendance officers or the LA attendance service to ensure that a pattern of non-attendance does not become entrenched.

2. **Pupils who have dropped out of school** should be referred to the Children Missing Education panel, which would consider strategies for re-integration or alternative placement.

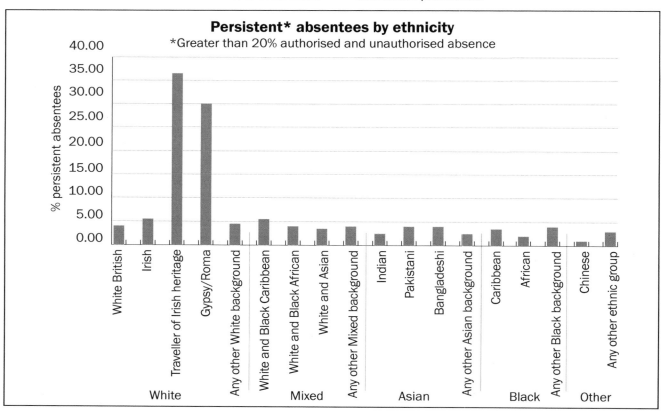

Persistent* absentees by ethnicity
*Greater than 20% authorised and unauthorised absence

3. **Pupils who have permanently moved away from the area** of the school are not truanting but may have to stay on roll until they appear on the roll of another school; this could take time due to family circumstances, how organised and proactive their access to TESS support and the availability of suitable school places in the area to which they have moved.

4. **Pupils who have temporarily moved away from the area**. Their parents may enrol their children in another school, but want their original place to be kept open; in such a case dual registration is possible and attendances at one school can be counted by the other.

5. **Pupils whose home circumstances make it difficult or impossible to attend regularly** require sensitive, multi-agency support to establish the circumstances to re-establish a positive attendance pattern. This group might include children who are caring for or supporting their parents in a culturally sanctioned and selfless way.

6. **Genuinely nomadic** pupils whose absences can be recorded with "T". Their parents may defend themselves against prosecution if their children have attended 200 sessions in the previous twelve months[22] (see chapter on Law). Families should be encouraged to use Distance Learning Materials or register with e-lamp (see chapter on Distance Learning).

A speedy, appropriate and consistent response to non-attendance is necessary to minimise the impact of poor attendance on the achievement and opportunities of Gypsy Roma Traveller pupils.

Push and pull

Within these categories there may also be push and pull factors; children may choose not to attend school because they can't access the curriculum, they don't feel safe or they always find themselves in trouble when they do go in. On the other hand there may be pull factors, like a subculture on their site which is critical of school attendance, opportunities for interesting work or social experience in the community or expectations on them from their families.

Staff of schools following up absences should be aware of these possibilities and, in the first instance, try to unpick all the reasons for non-attendance. The ubiquitous stomach pain or headache can conceal a multitude of other issues that may have practical and constructive means of redress. They may also reveal causes for concern that may otherwise be overlooked.

Encouraging better attendance

Partnership with parents

When pupils move away from the area, schools find it particularly frustrating if parents don't give any explanation to them, leaving them uncertain whether to keep the place open and frequently feeling their efforts have been wasted. Part of a developing dialogue between schools and parents needs to encourage them to share information about their plans. Most schools do not want to prevent families from being mobile, they just want to do what they can to support continuity of education. The default setting for most families is to share the minimum of information, understandable in the context of their history. In many cases they may not have the information to share; frequently they are responding to rapidly changing events and the purpose of moving may be to escape some threat.

Parents who are educationally disadvantaged themselves may find it difficult to understand how education is a cumulative process, undermined by frequent absence. Schools may find it difficult to understand why extended family responsibilities and community events should take priority over a child's learning. Mobility is often the elephant in the room; families hope they won't have to move and disrupt their children's education and schools tend not to have an educational model which involves an education put together in a number of different settings. Moving to a new place is frequently associated in the mind of the families with making a fresh start; not only are they reluctant to cooperate in their own surveillance, but also a sense of living in the present makes them reluctant to take with them information which links them to what they have put behind them. The gulf of understanding is substantial and can only be bridged through dialogue before the family moves.

Some families, particularly those travelling with circuses and fairgrounds, carry around a red book which each school can stamp when they enrol, so that subsequent schools can see where they had been previously and request records. S2S, the online system for schools' transfer educational records, can store the records of children whose subsequent school is not known, and has provided a similar function. But nothing can substitute relationships of trust built through respect and dialogue, supported by the national network of TESSs.

While we would encourage schools to be understanding of and sympathetic to the reasons why Gypsy Roma Traveller pupils attend poorly, we would not advocate tolerating poor attendance. The national attendance profile should make us more proactive, taking account of the context.

Using the legal process

Those of us who have been engaged in supporting the educational entitlement of Gypsy Roma Traveller children to education can find it difficult to see the law being used to compel families to send their children to school. Again, we have to take account of the

[22] s444 Education Act 1996.

complexity of the context to establish whether legal action is likely to result in the desired outcomes.

In some cases, where there is a subculture that is hostile to secondary school attendance, legal action has been successfully used to counterbalance social pressure and to support families who are committed to their children's education. Some families have a succession of children who drop out of school at the end of secondary; it is very hard to break the cycle as the younger siblings ask why they should go to school when their older brothers and sisters did not. "Because we'll be taken to court if you don't," is sadly an effective response.

It is important that decisions to prosecute are not taken by, but are taken in consultation with, Traveller Education specialists, with the sole aim of establishing whether this course of action is in the best interests of the child, and that there is no realistic alternative.

Partnership with Traveller Education professionals

As far as is possible the school, supported by the Local Authority attendance service, should address attendance issues. Traveller Education professionals are there to be consulted on the broader picture, the ECM context. Traveller Education professionals supporting attendance may be teachers, inclusion officers, attendance officers or home-school liaison officers. Usually they will be part of a TESS, but increasingly, as teams are mainstreamed, they may act as specialists within other teams. They are employed because these communities have historically been excluded from the education system and frequently become disengaged from it.

Educational engagement works best when Gypsy Roma Traveller families and schools talk directly to each other without a mediator. In our experience each side is more willing to give ground if they are talking face to face. Families have to explain their needs and schools must make their expectations transparent.

The role of Traveller Education professionals is supporting the establishment of this dialogue; families may be afraid to contact a school and the school may not have had the opportunity to welcome them. This is often the case when a family has newly arrived in an area or is highly mobile. But as soon as a relationship is established, the TEPs should begin to withdraw.

This, however, is not the end of their role. Not only do they remain available should circumstances change, but they will re-engage when families move, hit crises or are going through educational transitions. They can provide advice to the school on educational strategies, offer staff training and assist the school in celebrating Gypsy Roma Traveller History Month.

Many schools operate first day call to parents, which requires the school to keep up-to-date phone numbers. Many Travellers don't have landlines, and mobile numbers frequently change. Families should also understand the importance of having an emergency number in case anything happens to the child at school. TESSs, attendance services and schools need to inform each other if numbers change.

When families move TESSs can often contact other family or community members to try to establish where a family has gone and, through the national network of services, put the family in contact with someone who can support access to education in the area to which they have moved.

TESSs can support schools in emphasising the importance of informing schools when they are planning to leave. Families often travel in the summer months, or return to Eastern Europe before the end of term, when the flights are cheap, and schools need to know about such absences. They do interfere with children's education although they also have important educational, social and cultural value to the child and family. In practice, schools are more likely to keep a place open if a family makes the request directly, than they would be if the family just stopped attending or sent a message via the TESS. Schools often respond "This time, but not next time" or "OK, but can you make sure they attend every day when you come back?"

Pause for thought

• Do the parents understand that poor attendance seriously undermines learning and achievement?

• Do we make poor attendance an excuse for low attainment?

• Do we use encouragement and enforcement appropriately?

• Are all agencies singing from the same hymn sheet on attendance?

• Are child carers identified and sympathetically supported?

Support for transitions

Traveller Education Support Services usually maintain a database of all Gypsy Roma Traveller children and young people from birth to 19 living in or attending school in the area. In some cases they have a standalone system, but increasingly the information is kept on the local authority management information system. Children who are not yet in school, are between schools, have been excluded or have dropped out are the most vulnerable and most easily overlooked. Schools do a good job in supporting the attendance of the pupils on their rolls, but cannot reasonably be expected to take responsibility for those who are not yet, or no longer, on roll. The TESS has a critical role in ensuring that these children do not fall through the net of provision.

The information on the database is derived from a range of sources. Most TESSs have close links with their local Gypsy Roma and Traveller communities, established over a long period. They learn about new arrivals through family and community connections, referrals from schools, other agencies, voluntary and statutory, and from the national network of Traveller Education Services. Families known to the service will frequently phone us, and circus and fairground families contact us prior to their arrival. Some services use an outreach worker from the communities. The database is the primary means of recording and sharing information on Gypsy Roma Traveller children and families within the TESS and with other departments within Children Services.

The service uses the database to identify groups of children who may need support through transitions, specifically:

- families newly arrived in the LA

- families moving within the LA

- families leaving the LA

- families experiencing domestic difficulties which impact on their children's education

- families with children approaching nursery age

- families with children approaching compulsory school age

- families with children approaching secondary transfer

- young people choosing options at Key Stage 3, including alternative curriculum

- monitoring and supporting excluded children and young people to ensure they are not lost to the system

- young people moving into education, employment and training post-16.

Where Gypsy Roma Traveller learners are outside the education system, the TESS is usually the front-line agency promoting their access to the education system. When they are within the education system, our role is to monitor and support the work of schools and LA services such as Education Welfare and Connexions.

The TESS seeks to encourage Gypsy Roma Traveller parents, many of whom themselves had disadvantaged, disrupted or different educational experiences, to become active participants in the education process. Parents have anxieties about sending their children to secondary schools, citing issues of safety and relevance. To ensure all Gypsy Roma Traveller learners transfer to secondary schools the TESSs undertake a programme of home visits, starting a year before the scheduled transition. A suggested checklist of interventions is attached as Appendix I. The aim of these visits is to explain the process, allay anxieties and encourage parental choice.

In the same way, a programme of outreach is undertaken to inform parents about the availability of pre-school provision and the potential benefits to their child. There are high levels of mobility among many families, and it is important to lay firm foundations for later learning in the early years. Foundation Stage scores indicate that Gypsy Roma Traveller pupils have dropped below most other ethnic groups by the end of their first year of compulsory schooling, and pre-school experience provides an opportunity to minimise this disadvantage.

Children's Centres, as one-stop-shops for Children's Services with an outreach role to their localities, provide models of how mainstream services can take on an inclusive function with respect to vulnerable groups. TESSs work with them to ensure that Gypsy Roma Traveller families in their areas are aware of the provision, and Children Centres go the extra mile to encourage them to participate.

The TESS visits all families with children approaching nursery school age to explain the value of Early Years education and to identify appropriate local provision. Pre-school education is not compulsory and some families elect not to take up the offer; in Eastern Europe compulsory education starts later than in the UK and many Roma are reluctant to leave their children at this age. In such cases the service will also ensure they are visited again prior to their child reaching compulsory school age.

When families arrive in the LA the TESS supports

their access into schooling. EWS are informed at the outset and will consider taking legal action if families do not enrol their children in school. When a family leaves, the TESS will use its contacts within the communities and the national network of TESSs to try to establish where the family has gone and whether it is appropriate to take them off roll. If their whereabouts cannot be established, they will be placed on the missing children's register. There is a protocol (Appendix II) that clarifies the shared responsibilities of the TESS and EWS in supporting Gypsy Roma Traveller families who are mobile.

Retention of Gypsy Roma Traveller students at Key Stages 3 and 4 is a national concern. Every effort is made to engage students and their families in the choice of options for Key Stage 4 in order that their education should be relevant and appropriate to their aspirations. In some cases students pursue an alternative curriculum off-site and we have found that, if this transition is not carefully monitored, students can drop out of education while appearing to be on the roll of a school. The TESS works closely with schools to ensure that alternative curriculum placements are successful and provide routes to further education, training or employment.

Raising the achievement of Gypsy Roma Traveller pupils

Raising achievement in schools is currently mediated through the National Strategies. A huge amount of guidance and resources is published by the Strategies and it is not our purpose to replicate or summarise these publications. Our aim is to consider how the range of strategies has impacted on the achievement of Gypsy Roma Traveller pupils and, at a time of significant change, to consider the potential of strategies currently being introduced to address the continuing underachievement of vulnerable groups.

The National Strategies have changed the face of educational practice over the past decade. They have also changed themselves over that period, perhaps most graphically illustrated by widespread adoption of the literacy and numeracy hours and their subsequent replacement by the Primary Frameworks. It is important that not only do education policy and practice continue to change and develop but also that teachers take ownership of the process.

The current focus on personalisation and narrowing the gap is a response to recognition that, as general standards have improved, the 'long tail of under-achievement' has remained. This is of particular relevance to the education of Gypsy Roma Traveller pupils because most of them fall into that category.

The table below summarises a range of strategy interventions, their potential to benefit Gypsy Roma Traveller pupils, and our assessment of their effectiveness.

	Potential benefit	Effectiveness
Foundation stage profile	Systematic framework for assessing development and skills on which future learning will be based.	Lack of integration with Key Stage 1 curriculum, limited use made of identified areas to personalise learning.
Literacy hour	It emphasised the responsibility of schools to teach reading and writing and allocate a significant time to it, potentially of benefit to children from less literate homes.	Only the most inspirational teachers were able to engage children across a wide range of literacy experience. The rigid time frame fragmented learning, reducing relevance and enjoyment.
Numeracy hour	Stress on mental maths, use of range of strategies to reach objectives	The practically based problem-solving approach suited Gypsy Roma Traveller pupils, though they began to struggle towards the end of KS2.
Wave 2 (Small group intervention for children who can be expected to catch up with their peers as a result of the intervention)	Well-structured, focused, activity-based interventions had the capacity to ground basic skills, support catch-up and enable children to access the curriculum through appropriately differentiated quality first teaching.	Wave 2 interventions were a scarce resource and children identified were not always those most able to benefit. Gypsy Roma Traveller pupils tended to lose ground again, due to lack of engagement or other issues.
Wave 3 (Specific targeted intervention for children identified as requiring SEN support)	Targeted interventions aimed at addressing more serious learning difficulties.	Reading Recovery, the most expensive intervention, was the most successful, giving Gypsy Roma Traveller pupils skills which enabled them to access the curriculum. Talking partners gives confidence and helps structure learning.
Behaviour and attendance strands	Developing whole school policies to create an environment where learning is possible.	Greater engagement of schools with families and rapid response to absence. Some behaviour policies based on zero tolerance and internal exclusions improved whole school behaviour at the expense of personalised targets.

Multi-ethnic achievement programme	Leadership vision emphasising cultural difference not deficit; effective use of EAL staff across the curriculum.	Whole school ethos valuing diversity. Second adult to ensure curriculum accessible to all children. Specific relevance to EAL Roma pupils.
New arrivals Excellence programme	Range of strategies to welcome and include new arrivals.	Tending to focus on new arrivals from other countries, but appropriate strategies for inducting any mid-term admissions.

The National Strategies work on the assumption that children have a reasonably settled school experience. Understandably, schools may be reluctant to select children who do not attend regularly for intervention support. Pupils arriving mid-term may miss the opportunity of being assessed and offered intervention support and those who have had disrupted educational experiences may be below the skills level required to benefit from Wave 2 interventions. More worrying is the reluctance of schools to offer intervention support to mobile pupils on the basis that the resource might be wasted if the family moves on.

Having said that, we believe that the Strategies have played their part in the small improvement in Gypsy Roma Traveller achievement over the past five years. By systematically allocating time to the development of basic skills, schools began to compensate for the disadvantage of those children who didn't bring those skills from home. Wave 2 interventions swept up children who were falling behind their peers and Wave 3 interventions had the capacity to address more serious learning difficulties and deficits.

The improvement in Gypsy Roma Traveller achievement at Key Stage 2 has mirrored the improvement in all children, so the gap has not begun to close. The reason is that achievement is an Every Child Matters issue and can only be raised in the context of social inclusion and cohesion and economic and physical well-being (see chapter on Attendance and Every Child Matters).

Personalised Learning

Currently, personalised learning is the main show in town, with the capacity to raise the achievement of these groups. We'd like to examine its potential to address their educational needs.

The key document, 'personalised learning - a practical guide', describes Personalised learning as follows:

"The pedagogy of personalisation is distinguished by the way it expects all children and young people to reach or exceed national expectations, to fulfil their early promise and develop latent potential."

The ECM objective of reaching potential is brought together with the achievement objectives in this single, ambitious sentence. Reaching one's potential suggests uniqueness and diversity, but if this is judged only against national expectations its liberating connotations will be severely constrained. As we write, reform of the system of national testing is on the agenda of teachers' unions and the government, but the transitional nature of this guidance is evidenced by this sentence. Additionally, there is no acceptance of the difficulty involved in such an expectation. One of the principles of personalised learning is that children should be given achievable learning objectives; perhaps teachers should have achievable teaching objectives.

"Planning for progression and differentiation are fundamental. High expectations of progress apply equally to children and young people working above, at, or below age-related expectations, including those who have been identified as having special educational needs."

This should be of benefit to children with different or disrupted educational background, as well as the significant proportion of Gypsy Roma Traveller pupils on the Code of Practice.

"There is an expectation of participation, fulfilment and success; and teaching and learning is characterised by ambitious objectives, challenging personal targets, rapid intervention to keep pupils on trajectory and rigorous assessment to check and maintain pupil progress. There are clear plans to support those who are struggling to maintain trajectory."

Enjoyment seemed about to emerge, but was quickly overtaken by challenging targets and rigorous assessment.

The choice of a wheel to illustrate the pedagogy indicates how ambitious the project is.

Much of the previous section on reasons for underachievement falls into the single sector "Supporting children's wider needs". Virtually everything else can be addressed through school improvement and National Strategies support.

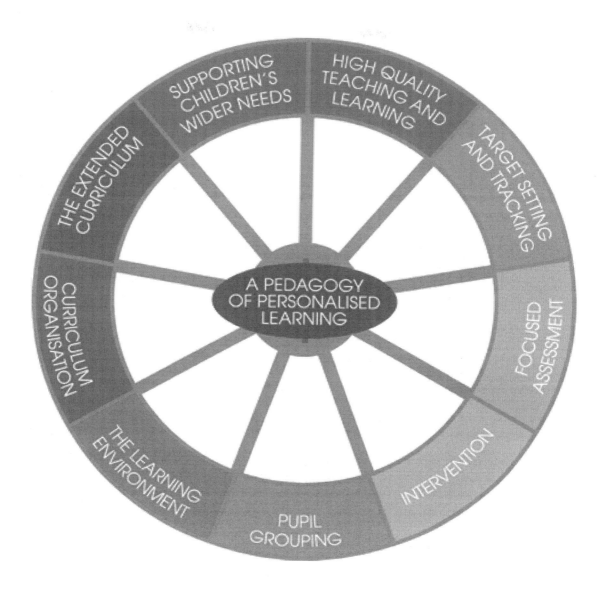

The model makes a lot of sense, and has great potential to support the learning and improve the outcomes of Gypsy Roma Traveller learners. In practice it represents a radical shift in the way schools work, and such changes require time, energy and commitment in order to be effectively implemented. Teachers will need to take ownership of the initiative, and we are concerned that they will need a great deal of support and encouragement in order for the changes to be effectively implemented.

Notwithstanding the challenge of implementation, notions of personalised learning are likely to influence practice in the years to come, and those who have a specific remit to improve the educational outcomes of Gypsy Roma Traveller communities will need to engage with and support their implementation. We propose to look at some of the initiatives and suggest how they have the potential to support Gypsy Roma Traveller achievement, and how they might undermine it.

Primary and Secondary frameworks

The new frameworks have, to judge from the descriptions on the Strategies website, a focus and purpose which should make a significant difference to vulnerable groups. They reduce prescription and encourage flexibility, engaging pupils in active, enquiry- based learning, focusing on key concepts and processes. The emphasis is on entitlement, inclusion and holding pupils into learning through high expectations, attention to prior learning and effective scaffolding and differentiation. The frameworks encourage cross-curricular links, the development of functional skills and learning for life. At a practical level, the frameworks integrate the curriculum, pedagogy and assessment methodology.

Assessment for Learning (AfL)

Many schools and teachers had begun to use Assessment for learning following the work of Shirley Clarke, Paul Black and Dylan William around the practical implementation of formative assessment. The basic principles are that pupils should be encouraged to assess their own learning through an understanding of learning objectives (what they are learning and why) through discussion stimulated by open questioning, through positive and constructive feedback and the opportunity to improve their work.

This approach is very powerful in stimulating the learning of Gypsy Roma Traveller pupils. Those whose parents were disadvantaged by their educational experiences may come into school unsure what the purpose of their education is. The frequently heard script, "You go to school to learn to read and write" leaves most of the curriculum untouched, and even lessons contributing to the ability to read and write may not have an obvious immediate connection.

Making the purpose of a lesson explicit immediately engages a child and challenges him or her to progress towards that objective, If that objective has relevance to the real world, daily life and the child's interests, so much the better. Each child's learning objectives should be achievable, ideally with some support from peers and adults; feedback and the opportunity to improve work done means the outcome can be successful. Through the process new learning objectives are identified.

Discussion and questioning play an important part in the process of providing opportunities for learners to develop their ideas and share them with their peers. Open questioning encourages all children to contribute, often giving them time for discussion with a partner first. It is inclusive, allowing children with different learning styles, knowledge and experiences to engage on equal terms. This approach more closely mirrors the learning styles of most Gypsy Roma Traveller pupils, building on discussion and oracy, rather than textbooks and correct answers. It suits the problem-solving approach that many Gypsy Roma Traveller pupils have. And it builds, rather than undermines, self-esteem.

Assessing pupil performance (APP)

Within the personalisation strategy AfL has become part of a three-level system, integrating formative with summative assessment.

- AfL provides the day-to-day information to inform short term planning and target setting at pupil level.

- APP is a system for monitoring the progression of a representative sample of children in the class.

- Transitional Assessments are the external assessments which may be made public and passed from phase to phase.

The selection of the representative sample within APP should ensure that quality first teaching is effectively differentiated to enable the range of children in a class to make progress. Because it is very detailed, it will provide much more reliable information to the teachers and subject leaders, enabling them to plan a differentiated curriculum and to identify appropriate candidates for interventions as well as monitoring the effectiveness of those interventions.

APP will use a range of evidence to assess pupil progress, including discussions with pupils, observations, written work and practical outcomes, as well as the views of other adults and parents. As such, it will form a well-rounded, evidence-based judgement of a pupil's education. If a Gypsy Roma Traveller pupil is selected as a marker child, an opportunity will be created to review how quality first teaching takes account of different Learning styles and experiences, cultural difference and parental engagement.

Behaviour, attendance and Social and Emotional Aspects of Learning (SEAL)

As pupils take ownership of their own learning, are able to achieve the learning objectives and receive positive feedback, it is hoped they will begin to enjoy and achieve and be motivated to attend school. But school must also be a place where they feel safe and respected for who they are, the patterns of behaviour they learned at home integrated with those expected by the school, and their parents encouraged to see how regular attendance is necessary for their children to achieve their full educational potential.

The personalisation agenda assumes children are attending school regularly; a well-differentiated curriculum cannot totally compensate for an educational experience that continues to be disrupted by absence.

SEAL is based upon Goleman's work on the importance of emotional intelligence and holds that social and emotional skills are at the heart of positive human development, effective social groups and societies, and effective education. It includes curriculum and whole school elements that can impact on the way all members of the school community relate to each other. Seven themes address issues such as relationships, bullying, identity, motivation and responding to changes. The key social and emotional aspects of learning - empathy, self-awareness, social skills and motivation – are explored through each theme.

Pupils from Gypsy and Irish Traveller backgrounds are encouraged to think of themselves as young adults and, although they show respect for their elders within the community, they are also accustomed to speaking to them as equals. This approach can be regarded by some teachers as rude and confrontational, when in practice it may not be. SEAL recognizes that

> "If school staff are to be able to help pupils develop social and emotional skills, then they need these skills too. Such skills inform professional competence as well as learning since teaching is fundamentally a social activity, demanding high levels of emotional sensitivity, good self-management, empathy and the ability to make relationships."

A consistent and positive response to behaviour has a major part to play in creating an environment where social and emotional skills can flourish. SEAL recognises that the underlying causes of difficult behaviour or persistent absence are often emotional or social, and addressing these, rather than the behavioural manifestations, is more likely to promote resolution and avoid exclusion. Absence may be due to causes such as fear of bullying, feelings of isolation, anxiety and lack of motivation or engagement with learning.

SEAL has the potential to create an inclusive environment in which pupils and staff respect and value each other, where the expected behaviour patterns are made explicit and embedded through the curriculum and the behaviour of staff.

Chris Derrington[23] has recently described the adaptations of Gypsy Roma Traveller pupils to school as "fight, flight or play white." She argues that many Gypsy Roma Traveller pupils are absent, aggressive or deny their identities as responses to racist abuse and bullying. SEAL provides clear policy frameworks for staff and pupils to address bullying, respect identity, build self-esteem and develop strategies for conflict resolution.

Other strategy initiatives

The National Strategies' Gypsy Roma Traveller Achievement programme objectives are:

- To improve outcomes for Gypsy Roma Traveller pupils, including narrowing of achievement gaps, through building capacity and sustainability at LA and school level.

- To ensure that the needs and educational aspirations of Gypsy Roma Traveller communities and their children are realised and expanded through effective personalised learning.

- To support the development of inclusive schools, including the promotion of race equality and the strategic management of mobility.

- To improve the knowledge and understanding of the unique cultural and educational issues relating to Gypsy Roma Traveller communities with local authorities, schools and other partners.

- To tailor established mainstream resources and guidance to address LA and school priorities relating to Gypsy Roma Traveller pupils' attainment.

The project involved twelve local authorities in its first two years, and has been extended to involve an additional twelve. Schools and LAs are expected to audit their provision for these groups and make action plans outlining their strategies for addressing the objectives above.

Good practice emerging includes focuses of parental engagement and participation, curriculum and attendance. National guidance on good practice will be published in Autumn 2009.

There is no doubt that encouraging schools to focus on the issues affecting Gypsy Roma Traveller achievement in their context has been very valuable in helping these schools to be creative and make sustainable changes to their practice. Much of the practice mirrors that encouragement in "Aiming High: Raising the Achievement of Gypsy Traveller Pupils", which was itself based on existing good practice developed by TESSs. The main difference is that the schools take the lead and therefore they feel greater ownership of the outcomes.

Gypsy Roma Traveller Achievement Programme supports only four schools in each LA and these have tended to be those with most Gypsy Roma Traveller pupils (often serving official sites) and most positive attitudes to developing practice in this area. The practice being developed has tended to reflect improved relationships between schools and local Gypsy Roma Traveller communities, relying less than previously on the mediating role of the TESS. This

[23] Derrington, C. (2007) Fight, Flight and Playing White: an examination of coping strategies adopted by Gypsy Traveller students in English Secondary Schools. International Journal of Educational Research 46(6), 357-367.

more direct relationship has raised the levels of mutual understanding and respect. The published DVD illustrates only primary schools and there is some evidence that secondaries have been more reluctant to participate.

Narrowing the gaps

From April 2009 there were significant changes in the focus of the Department for Children Schools and Families and the National Strategies. The DCSF Ethnic Minority Achievement Unit has become the Narrowing the Gaps department, reflecting the recognition that greatest under-attainment is not by gender, race or language status, but poverty. The gap between free school meal pupils and their peers is at least double that for any main census ethnic minority group. As a result, several achievement programmes targeting the "main" ethnic minorities are being brought to an end or consolidated into the Primary EAL programme. The Gypsy Roma Traveller Achievement programme will continue because of the size of the gap and its failure to close.

The achievement of ethnic minorities will now be encouraged by means of Local Authority target setting. One of the seven ethnic minority target groups is Gypsy Roma Travellers, and authorities are obliged to set a target if the cohort size is greater than three. Of necessity, the targets will be based only on the achievement of those children who ascribe, and with small cohorts it is inevitable that achieving LA targets will result on a focus on ascribed children with the potential to cross achievement thresholds, rather than on the whole group. In addition LAs are required to set targets for the achievement of children on free school meals (as an indicator of poverty). This group will also include many Gypsy Roma Traveller pupils, but target-setting is unlikely to be effective unless it is associated with political initiatives to address child poverty. There is a danger that Gypsy Roma Traveller achievement may, in remaining as a stand-alone ethnic minority achievement programme, become marginalised within the closing the gap agenda.

Pause for thought

• Is there a clear assessment policy to ensure that newly-arrived pupils receive appropriate personalised support as quickly as possible?

• Does access to intervention support discriminate in favour of or against children with different and/or disrupted educational experiences?

• How does personalisation address culture, identity and learning style?

• Do the children and their parents feel ownership of their achievement?

• Does the TESS have a clear role in raising achievement?

Distance Learning for Traveller Children

Distance Learning programmes have been in place for some children from Circus and Fairground families for many years now and much has been learned about how to manage this way of working successfully.

Distance Learning as practised by most Traveller Education Services tends to start from the assumption that the children are both mobile and have a regular school base that they will return to each year. A programme that carries on in the travelling months follows on the heels of learning that takes place in the winter. When children return to school in the winter they should feel that they have not missed too much while they have been away. The teaching staff should not have so much catch-up work to do. When these programmes are successfully managed, it is possible for school attendance to be maintained by awarding attendance marks for 'education off site'.

Where children are moving from one site to another and are not mobile, it is better to consider 'dual registration' with the child enrolled in two schools who communicate with each other and share the teaching at different times of year. Where children do not have a regular school base, this virtuous cycle is impossible to maintain because no individual has the oversight of the child's learning and progress. The child needs feedback about performance and the quality of work and the learning programme needs to be carefully structured. The E-lamp programme administered by the National Association of Teachers of Travellers has recently introduced a B strand to provide for the needs of disaffected children who have a regular home base but who are not enrolled in school.

This programme provides the pupils with a laptop and access to online courses and is designed to be supported by local Traveller Education Service teachers on a part-time basis. It remains to be seen whether this programme provides real opportunities for young people in Years 10 and 11 or simply salves consciences and gives the impression that 'something is being done'. It is a matter of debate within Traveller Education teams as to whether these programmes really make 'every child matter' or add weight to the inclusive argument that all education outside the mainstream is impoverished.

The dilemma is that while the DCSF supports mainstreaming, it also supports the E-Lamp strand B which is definitely not mainstreaming. But TESSs participating in the Strand B programme have been able to re-engage some young people who would not otherwise have been reached. In many ways this programme highlights the tensions and dilemmas that exist between Every Child Matters and Mainstreaming.

By working through Distance Learning we can develop confident independent learners who return to school ready to pick up where they left off. The regular communication with their teachers, teaching assistants and friends creates a feeling of belonging that can overcome the fear of returning to school after a long and often unexplained absence.

The children who have been following the Distance Learning programme feel a greater connection and sense of belonging to the school, and their attendance patterns are more fully understood by the whole of the school community. If the programme has been well designed and followed by the child and the family, continuity of learning has been facilitated and maintained. Schools that achieve this demonstrate that for them "Every Child Matters".

Planning Distance Learning is really about devising a personalised learning programme. Each programme is likely to be designed in a different way, although it is perfectly possible to use the same learning materials within programmes designed for different children.

In recent years computers and mobile connectivity to the internet have been available, for use by children and their families, to Traveller Education Services participating in the E-Lamp programme. Although this programme will soon come to an end, the planned roll out of computers and broadband connections to all vulnerable children in their homes through the Home Access to ICT for Targeted Groups initiative should ensure that access is continued and extended. Gypsy, Roma and Traveller pupils are included in the list of potential beneficiaries who LAs can include in their bids.

When planning Distance Learning, it is vital to understand the mobility patterns and living arrangements of the children and their families. If these are not fully understood, it is likely that the programme will fail. All families are different, but what they have in common is that travelling and work are intimately connected. One or both parents may have to work for some or part of the day and evening. Bedtimes may need to be moved so that the family are late to bed and late to rise. Some days may be entirely given over to moving from one place to another, others may have an hour or so when children can work and be supervised by parents. Yet other days may be quite settled with more prolonged periods when children can get on with their learning pack. It is through discussion with parents that these vital details will come to be understood and the early structure of the pack can begin to be designed.

How many minutes or hours (preferably not more than two hours a day plus reading time for older secondary school pupils) a day will the child work? How much supervision can the parent achieve? What resources are most suitable for this child? If there is a laptop computer available, will the parents be able to re-charge the battery? Is there a mobile internet connection available? Is the family likely to be in an area where there is a good quality mobile phone signal? How can you make the best use of the technology? Will you give the child access to the schools learning platform? Is e-mail the best solution? Is there a role for Traveller Education Services and if so what is that role?

Once this discussion has taken place, a learning agreement can be implemented and each participant can agree:
• the time to be spent on the programme;

• the way in which the programme will be supervised by the parents.

A strategy for communication detailing:
• who will initiate the communication;

• who will be kept informed;

• frequency of communication;

• who should work be returned to? (This is more complex in a secondary school than in a primary)

• Who will set work?

• How often?

• How will returned work be assessed?

• How will assessments be returned to pupils?

• What will happen if work is being returned late?

• Are dates for departure from school and return to school known? Or when will they be known?

Preparing the materials

Distance Learning needs to be broken down into small achievable blocks that form the work for an identifiable

period of time. For example, "This is three hours of Maths work that must be returned by the 10th June" or "This is five hours of English work that you should return by the end of next week". The pupils should always be encouraged to report back on each unit of work:
• How long did the work actually take to complete?

• Were there any difficulties and have these been resolved?

• Are there any questions from the pupil?

• Was the unit pitched at the correct level?

• What was interesting, enjoyable or tedious?

I remember visiting an angry mother on site once who had a carrier bag full of worksheets for each of her children. None of the family knew what they should tackle first. If mum marked the work the children said, "You're not my teacher. That's not the way my teacher does it." When the children returned to school in the autumn they were in new classes with new teachers and they got no feedback from the work they had completed. They all felt that they were being kept occupied and not that they were learning and making progress.

The learning packs should include all the materials that the child will need. If you are asking for work to be returned regularly, then the children will need to work on paper or in booklets or online. Exercise books are clumsy to return and their loss leaves the child with nothing to work in until they are returned. What will happen when the work is returned? Will more be available and how soon?

Finally, the tasks should be safe to complete within the home environment. On one occasion I was delighted to hear that a Science teacher had set practical work for a Year 7 pupil, but when I went to visit home I found that the parents were very upset as the pupil had been asked to use a candle with an open flame in a caravan, which is a very flammable environment.

Attendance for Traveller pupils is a very thorny issue as schools are set exacting targets for good attendance. The authorised absence mark that Traveller children are awarded when they are travelling does not support the school in achieving its attendance target. However, headteachers can set up Distance Learning programmes and ensure that parents are prepared by the school and the Local Authority and deemed competent to supervise their children's learning. If the Distance Learning is returned and the Head is satisfied that it is being correctly followed, then a "B" can be awarded in the register. This is an education off-site mark and counts as an attendance.

At the end of the Travelling period a debriefing should take place. How did each of the parties find the programme? What went well? What was difficult? Was the work repetitive for the child or was it interesting and exciting? Can anyone see an effective way of improving the system for next year? Above all, if the child did not complete the learning programme, why was this? Can the issue be resolved?

When the parents, the children and the school are all working together towards shared goals, Distance Learning offers great potential for enhancing the education of Traveller pupils, but it is not simple if done well. It requires a great deal of careful planning and follow up, especially when the child is away travelling.

Elective Home Education

The European Convention on Human Rights (ECHR) Article 2 of Protocol 1 states:

"No person shall be denied the right to education. In the exercise of any functions which it assumes in relation to education and to teaching, the State shall respect the right of parents to ensure such education and teaching is in conformity with their own religious and philosophical convictions."

A child has a right to be educated, but the parents have the right to ensure that that education is in accordance with their beliefs. The state provides an education system to serve the needs of that right, but also has a responsibility to ensure its citizens respect a child's right to education. Citizens whose values do not chime with those of the State, those who think they can do a better job than the state system and those whose children have had bad experiences in formal education, may wish to educate their children in a way which reflects their own beliefs and attitudes. The State, as the upholder of human rights, must judge whether the education provided by self-educators conforms to a shared understanding of a good education. Here lies a tension and an irresolvable dilemma; how can those who provide state education judge the provision made by those who have consciously rejected the state model.

In many cases the self-educators are well educated, well able to critique the state system and design an alternative; if the State wants to take issue with their provision and content, they can give as good as they get. To most local authorities, home-educators represent an idiosyncratic minority and are looking after themselves; in practice, their children may disengage and re-engage with mainstream education at various points in their educational careers and show no signs of being damaged or short-changed by the process.

In January 2009, the DCSF, commissioned Graham Badman, the former Managing Director of Children Schools and Families Service in Kent, to conduct a review on Elective Home Education in England , with a particular focus on safeguarding issues and ways to strengthen the existing arrangements. The review exposed the limitations on the powers of local authorities to hear the views of home-educated children and establish whether their right to education was being denied. The report did not refer to the particular situation of Gypsy Roma Travellers, but it made twenty-eight recommendations, the key ones of which are as follows.

1. A compulsory national registration scheme, locally administered, for all children of statutory school age, who are, or become, electively home educated.

Registration would be renewed annually and home educators must provide a clear statement of their educational approach, intent and desired/planned outcomes for the child over the following twelve months

2. A review of the current statutory definition of what constitutes a "suitable" and "efficient" education to ensure that home-educated children and young people have sufficient information to enable them to expand their talents and make choices about likely careers.

3. Designated and trained local authority officers should:
   - have the right of access to the home;
   - have the right to speak with each child alone, or with a trusted adult who is not the home educator.

   Parents would be required to allow their children to demonstrate their achievements and progress.

4. Local authorities should offer a menu of support to home educating families in accord with the requirements placed upon them by the power of wellbeing, extended schools and community engagement and other legislation.

At the time of writing this report is subject to consultation at *http://www.dcsf.gov.uk/consultations/*

Gypsy Roma Travellers and Elective Home Education

Some Gypsy, Roma and Irish Traveller families are also sceptical of state education. They feel that gorgios, buffers, country people, whoever – them, not us – are trying to impose their values on their children. In so far as successful education in our society seems to be defined by five or more A* to C grades at GCSE, through university education to the professions, and since few Gypsy Roma Traveller parents aspire for their children to enter the professions, one can understand the origin of their scepticism. In addition, parents are concerned that their children may learn things in school (both formally and informally) that they do not wish them to learn (for example, sex, drugs and foreign languages) while they could be learning life skills in their communities which would equip them to survive and prosper as adults.

At a more pragmatic level, children and young people make an important contribution to the life of their family, caring for siblings, helping with chores and contributing to the family business. The home is a place of safety in contrast to what they perceive to be an increasingly threatening world. Although Gypsy

Roma Traveller communities don't arrange marriages, most parents have ideas about who would make an appropriate partner for their child; keeping secondary age children at home makes it possible for parents to have control over their social lives.

In some cases parents register for EHE because they have high aspirations; they feel that if their children are to engage with education they want the best outcomes, and therefore wish their children to enrol in what they see as the best schools. Such schools are often over-subscribed, have complex entry requirements that are easy to fall foul of, or the family is in the wrong place at the wrong time. In other cases families reluctantly opt for EHE because their children's educational needs are not being met by their school, but they remain willing to re-engage if an appropriate curriculum offer can be identified.

New Traveller families frequently home educate. In most cases their children are well provided for because the parents are themselves educated and their lifestyle presents a broad range of educational opportunities. Such families may also re-engage with mainstream education if their circumstances change, or their children require a curriculum and qualifications provided in schools and colleges.

Until quite recently Gypsy Roma Traveller parents who did not want their children to attend secondary school opted out of the secondary transfer process. They had observed that they were more likely to be chased by attendance officers if their children were on roll but not attending well, than if they were not on the roll of any school. Recently, schools have begun to monitor the return of applications for secondary school places and contact parents who have not made an application. TESSs also adopt proactive strategies to encourage parents to engage with the secondary transfer process (see checklist). Even those parents who said their children had gone to stay with extended family members in other parts of the country or in different countries have been expected to give details of where their children are being educated and who is responsible for them.

In contrast, families registering their children for EHE have found themselves in a relatively protected position. LAs responding to Badman expressed their dissatisfaction with the current legislative position and guidance, which many found unworkable. "In particular, the absence of a more precise definition of what constitutes a "suitable" and "efficient" education militates against benchmarked attainment and being denied access to the place of education, and the opportunity to speak with the child, prevents them from fulfilling their current statutory duties.." [25]

The DfES commissioned an in-house survey of the workings of EHE with particular reference to Gypsy Roma Travellers. Questionnaires were sent to the TESS and to the person with responsibility for EHE in twenty-three authorities.[26] This survey found that the most common reason given by parents for electing to home educate was fear of cultural erosion and lack of cultural relevance. In addition, parents had concerns about the educational philosophy of the school and racist bullying.[27] Gypsy Roma Traveller parents are most concerned that education will undermine their culture and their children will not be equipped by schools to survive as Traveller adults. It is likely that concerns around educational philosophy relate to sex education and gender stereotyping.

The Ivatts report concluded that:

"The developments described within this report provide clear evidence that Gypsy, Roma and Traveller communities represent a unique case. Because of inherent inadequacies within mainstream educational provision as listed, it could be argued that increasing numbers of children from these communities are unjustly being 'removed' de facto from mainstream provision. And yet these are the communities most ill placed to organise or deliver an efficient and suitable education for their children. Many parents have very low level literacy skills, have limited and negative experiences of attending school themselves and are among the least qualified to be able to make a sound and informed judgement on the quality of the education that they are managing to provide or organise for their children. There is little doubt that few Gypsy/Roma and Traveller parents are providing their children with a suitable education. As either consumers or providers parents are thus seriously disadvantaged."

Education Otherwise, an organisation which supports home education, made the following robust response to this report.

"EO expressed strong distaste for this ethnic group being singled out as different in the eyes of the law from any other home educating families. The DfES has apparently had representations from these communities saying that they experience racial and cultural prejudice at local authority level, which is why the draft Guidelines include a recommendation that there should be referral or engagement with the local Traveller Education Service.

However EO made the point that the TESS has a strong ethos of inclusion and re-integration into the school system and that therefore this is

[25] op.cit p15, para 5.1

[26] Ivatts, A. (2006). The Situation Regarding the Current Policy, Provision and Practice in Elective Home Education (EHE) for Gypsy, Roma and Traveller children. London: DfES

[27] TESSs were significantly more likely to identify this as a cause than LA officials.

inappropriate for Traveller Gypsy Roma families who categorise themselves as electively home educating and for whom the EHE department is the correct point of reference as for all other home educating families of whatever ethnic background. " [28]

The current DCSF guidance[29] includes a single paragraph suggesting that local authorities should have an understanding of, and be sensitive to, the distinct ethos and needs of Gypsy, Roma and Traveller communities. "It is important that these families who are electively home educating are treated in the same way as any other families." It then suggests the involvement of the TESS for advice and access to local settings.

One of the main dilemmas in assessing the efficiency of the education provided arises because home educators are not required to follow the national curriculum or even provide a broad and balanced curriculum. There need be no timetable or contact time, and the educators need no educational qualifications. Local Authorities do not have the duty to monitor EHE but they do have a responsibility to make sure all children receive a suitable education. In practice they can ask parents for evidence that their children are receiving education and if that evidence is unsatisfactory the LA can seek a school attendance order. Even where a school attendance order is issued, families may place the children in school for a few terms and then re-register for EHE starting the process all over again.

From a community perspective Gypsies and Irish Travellers have prepared their children for adult life by giving them responsibility from an early age and having their children work alongside them as they go about their daily work. In practice this has resulted in most young men having the skills and resources to earn a living by the time they are 16 or 17. They will share the proceeds of the work they do, and young men may have enough money to buy a trailer and establish a home around the time they plan to get married. Not only do families feel that this is a more reliable way of safeguarding their future than relying on formal education, paper qualifications and job centres, but they feel that schooling may blunt the edge of their initiative and enterprise. In addition, there are strongly held cultural and religious values relating to sex education and opposed to premarital relationships, which many Gypsy Roma Travellers feel are undermined by secondary school attendance. By opting for EHE they feel their culture is strengthened and safeguarded. So EHE enables them to bring up their children in a traditional way, without their culture and values being undermined by the values of settled society.

[28] Notes of meeting with DfES JUNE 22nd 2007

[29] DCSF(2007) Elective Home Education Guidance

On the downside, the options for girls are particularly limited by this arrangement. They are likely to take an increasing amount of responsibility for the care of children and the home, until they marry and take responsibility for their own home and family. Although it is the religious and cultural norm to assume that marriages will succeed, some marriages fail, leaving women with little formal education and few options for making provision for themselves and their families. Induction into the family business works well when fathers have sufficient work, but increasing numbers of men have only occasional and casual work, and no longer have a trade to pass onto their sons. Educational limitations restrict business opportunities for the communities; increasingly subcontractors are expected to be registered and comply with Health and Safety regulations. Most of the employment opportunities will be in the grey or black economies, often without legal safeguards or redress, and at low rates of pay. Having said that, we have to concede that in the current climate most educational qualifications do not guarantee employment and the aspirational target of five plus A* to C grades at GCSE (with English and Maths) offers no certainty of economic prosperity.

Finally, official sites, especially those which are isolated from other communities, frequently develop a sub-culture which is hostile to secondary school attendance. Parents and children who attend secondary school are treated as stupid at best, culturally treacherous at worst, and an anti-school ethos gathers momentum. In such a context, opting for EHE may be not so much a culturally appropriate choice as a response to social pressure.

Implications for practice

Each Local Authority is expected to identify a senior officer with responsibility for monitoring Elective Home Education.

- This person should have a discussion with LA staff responsible for supporting Traveller Education to establish how the policies and practices in the authority should be applied to Gypsy Roma Traveller families.

- Schools need to be clear about what steps they should take if a family seeks to register for EHE.

- The policy needs to be clear about time-scales and acceptable levels of proof and the steps which will be taken if the provision is not acceptable.

- Although Gypsy Roma Traveller families should be treated like anyone else, there needs to be an understanding that Gypsy Roma Traveller parents may be less equipped to deliver a suitable education than other home educators.

- The TESS needs to remain in contact with home educating parents and identify ways in which they can re-engage with education to supplement or replace EHE.

- Although the adoption of EHE by an increasing number of families may seem to undermine much of the work done by TESSs over the past decades, it should also be seen as a challenge to the education system. We have yet to convince many Gypsy Roma Traveller families that schools provide an education which meets the needs of their community and culture, in an environment which is safe and affirming.

The Work of Traveller Education Support Services: *Evaluating Practice*

"Our emphasis on narrowing the gaps recognises that gaps arise more from differences in children's backgrounds than from what happens within school. Gaps are affected by the aspirations of the pupils themselves, their parents and their communities, their home learning environment and their ability to access support from other services. So our approach cannot be based solely on improving what schools do in the classroom. We must also engage young people and build their confidence; encourage parents to become more involved with their children's learning; change community perceptions of the value of education; and enable schools to play their full part within their local Children's Trust."

Geoff Brown DCSF "From Aiming High to Narrowing the Gaps" Ethnic Minority Achievement Programme newsletter: Spring 2009.

Narrowing the gaps between underachieving groups and other children has become a key focus of government policy and intervention in recent years. Narrowing the gaps in education, and the aspects of families lives which affect entitlement, has been the raison d'étre of TESSs since their inception. In this chapter we describe the ways services seek to do this. For some time now the DCSF has acknowledged that to adequately support children, especially those seen as vulnerable, it requires multi-agency collaborative working. This has been in line with the efforts by government to find 'joined up' solutions to the issues of social exclusion through promoting the development of policy that offers strategic solutions and promotes interagency working. The Laming report into the death of Victoria Climbié further reinforced the need for multi-agency working and led to the publication of Every Child Matters and the formation of the five outcomes for all children.

The Every Child Matters agenda and subsequent Children Act 2004 promoted whole system change, with a particular emphasis on integrated working and bringing together schools, health, play and sports providers to ensure that healthy growth and development is happening in all areas of a child's life. In all of this the voice of the community and, in particular, the voice of the child is to be heard and opportunities given for participation in the decision-making processes.

At the same time, there has been a national campaign to raise achievement in schools with target-setting for schools to "raise the bar". This has created tensions between the standards and inclusion debates in many schools and has sometimes led to schools' feeling that the inclusion of Traveller children holds them back from achieving their attendance and attainment targets.

SEG = Socio-Economic Group

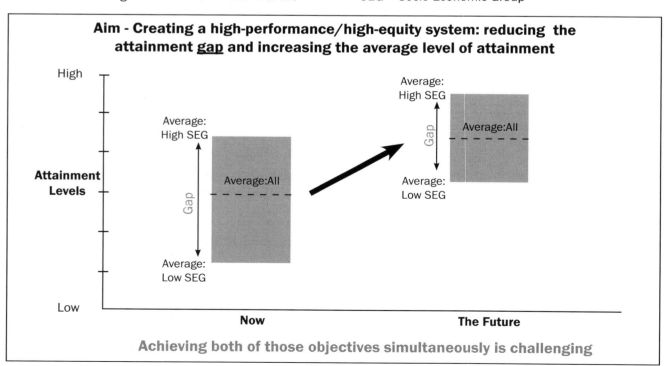

Aim - Creating a high-performance/high-equity system: reducing the attainment gap and increasing the average level of attainment

Achieving both of those objectives simultaneously is challenging

During National Strategy briefings the DCSF has laid out its intention to both raise standards and Narrow the Gap in Achievement for all children, in particular Gypsy Roma Traveller pupils. The chart on the previous page is taken from a DfES presentation on raising attainment from 2006.

Recent initiatives, Narrowing the Gap[30] and The Extra Mile pilot from the Child Poverty Unit, offer guidance on the evidence-based approaches that have been shown to effect significant change for vulnerable children. It is particularly interesting that each of these programmes identifies a series of actions that are similar, but not the same. Narrowing the Gap[31] is the title of a major two-year research and development project which is funded by the DCSF, hosted by the Local Government Association (LGA) and supported by the Improvement and Development Agency for local government (IDA). Its over-riding purpose is to make a significant difference, on a national scale, to the performance of Children's Trusts in narrowing the gap in outcomes between vulnerable and excluded children and the rest, against a context of improving outcomes for all.

This project (which is ongoing) focuses on families, Children's Centres, schools and other services and local authorities. At the end of its first year a series of ten hypotheses were identified about 'what works' in narrowing the gap, drawing out the factors that appear to be commonalities across all the templates.

We have used these "golden threads" as section headings to describe how TESSs work. The headings are: You can do it!, Together with Parents, Through the eyes of a child, Holding the baton, Learning to learn, Cornflakes to canoeing; United to succeed, Shape up and keep fit, Prove it, From good to great.

Closer analysis raises some questions and offers some ways forward for the way in which a range of services can offer support to Gypsy Roma Traveller pupils and their families.

Narrowing the Gap for Gypsy Roma Traveller pupils

Narrowing the Gap has, through consultation and research consisting of case studies, data collection, literature review, and mixed methods, identified key actions and it asserts that:

"These ten golden threads have to be taken together, applied universally and pursued relentlessly to achieve significant change. In other words, they are not a 'pick and mix list' but a recipe for whole system change."[32]

This tenacity and relentlessness characterise the work of TESS and many of the specific recommendations will be very familiar to TESS workers.

Some Gypsy Roma Traveller families access education independently, have good relationships with their children's schools and support their children's learning. The children of these families are more likely to stay on in school and achieve well.[33] This group is growing in number and effectiveness, but remains a minority. The purpose of Traveller Education Support Services is to support schools and families to develop independent relationships which will support their children's achievement, opportunities and equalities.

There are many reasons why children from Gypsy Roma Traveller heritages may underachieve.
• disrupted educational experience

• different educational experiences

• educational disadvantage of their parents

• social and economic reasons

• health reasons

• cultural reasons

• dispersed extended family demands

• lack of cultural sensitivity within the education system

• racism in employment sector

• lack of role models

• EAL issues

• accommodation issues

• refugee and asylum seeker issues.

These factors are not unique to Gypsy Roma Traveller families, but most families experience a number of them, often inter-acting with each other to undermine the families' ability to reach their full potential.

The role of TESS is to build the capacity of families, schools and other agencies, including the LA, to address these issues. In some cases a watching brief

[30] LGA, DCSF, and I&DA using research from NFER, 2008.

[31] Local Government Association (2008) http://www.lga.gov.uk/lga/core/page.do?pageId=234484.

[32] ibid

[33] Derrington, C. & Kendall, S. (2004). Gypsy Traveller students in secondary schools: culture, identity and achievement. Stoke on Trent, UK and Sterling USA: Trentham Books. (ISBN 1 85056 320 8).

may be sufficient, while in others complex inter-agency interventions may be required. There are many parallels with the situation of Looked After Children, where the need for a virtual headteacher has been recognised to pull together a range of professionals who might be working with a child.

You can do it!
("Expect the best")

This section recommends that parents, extended family, carers and all those in contact with children work together to create self-belief in all children.

Schools do a good and improving job supporting the achievement of Gypsy Roma Traveller pupils on roll, and frequently support families through phase transitions. S2S, the on-line record transfer system, has improved continuity for pupils moving from school to school. The National Strategies have developed interventions to enable children to catch up and Assessment for Learning ensures that children are working at an appropriate level, understand what they are learning and why.

Most Gypsy Roma Traveller children who have settled school experience and no Special Education Needs make at least two National Curriculum levels progress between Key Stages 1 and 2, although many are working below the expected levels. Unfortunately, a high proportion have disrupted school experience or are on the Code of Practice for SEN. TESS, who are part of school improvement services, contribute to a range of LA support for schools to extend good practice. The work of the TESS is to monitor and support pupils' learning, and often to be the supportive adult who assists them to negotiate the world of school and manage difficult transitions.

All children aspire to achieve success in their lives. Education professionals already play an important part by identifying the potential of young people, helping them to articulate and achieve their ambitions, and engaging their families. However by working collaboratively with parents and extended family and a wide range of other professionals, for example in the arts, sport and business, it will be possible to open up wider opportunities in the future.

The Average Child

I don't cause teachers trouble,
My grades have been ok.
I listen in my classes
And I'm in school everyday.

My teachers think I'm average,
My parents think so too.
I wish I didn't know that
'Cause there's lots I'd like to do.

I'd like to build a rocket, I have
A book that tells you how,
Or start a stamp collection—well
There's no use in trying now.

'Cause since I found I'm average
I'm just smart enough you see,
To know there is nothing special
That I should expect of me.

I'm part of the majority,
That hump part of the bell,
Who spends their life unnoticed
In an average kind of hell.

Mike Buscemi.

TESS support the development of a 'can do' culture by working to demonstrate that Traveller children's education is important both in schools and within Traveller communities, and they will be creative and imaginative in devising ways of enabling the children to be supported in accessing provision. This will demonstrate to children that they are important to us and we care about their futures. It is the ability to work with colleagues in school, the local authority and other services, as well as directly with children and families, which provides specialist staff with insights enabling the development of creative responses to enable Gypsy Roma Traveller pupils to succeed.

Together with Parents
("You know your child, we know children's services, we can help the child together")

In the case of Gypsy Roma Travellers the TESS frequently takes a key worker role, signposting the family to other services and building the awareness of those services through training and partnership working. Gypsy Roma Travellers have historically tended to fall through the net of provision; TESSs were established because the Plowden Committee recognised that focused interventions were necessary if these communities were to be engaged. Although the achievement of Gypsy Roma Travellers is a cause for national concern, many families are now engaged in education from pre-school to post-16. These levels of engagement are achieved through establishment of good relationships with families, partnership and liaison with education providers and a network of TESSs to minimise the disruption caused by mobility.

TESSs remain important in a number of other areas where schools do not, and cannot reasonably be expected to, have a remit. TESSs identify Gypsy Roma Traveller families living in, arriving in and moving within the LA area. Many of the most mobile families are also the most marginalised and disengaged; they do not automatically attempt to enrol their children in school, and if they do they may experience difficulties identifying places and meeting the requirements of the school. These are skills which families can learn, but they cannot be taken for granted. Newly arrived families may have a range of needs and education may not be their first priority; if families are distressed and disoriented, keeping their children close may be a natural response.

We must be honest: many Gypsy Roma Traveller families remain unconvinced of the value of secondary education. They were excluded from education for many years and have developed systems of self-education which prepare their children for the roles they anticipate they will have in adult life. There is a feeling that formal education will not only prevent children learning these important life skills, but also equip them with skills which might undermine the culture. For some families, not going to secondary school is a key marker of cultural identity. These values can be particularly strongly held on large official sites where an anti-school counter-culture develops. HMI (Her Majesty's Inspectorate) has recognised that an increasing number of Gypsy Roma Traveller families are registering for Elective Home Education, for reasons discussed in the chapter on EHE.

Through the eyes of a child

Gypsy Roma Traveller cultures are built around the support of and responsibilities to the extended family and community. Children are a part of their own unique families but are also a valued part of a much wider extended family and community. New Traveller children, who may seem to be from very small single parent families, can be part of an extensive network of supportive family, community and friendship groups.

These networks of family and friends are strengths, rather than hindrances, but often the family itself is under pressure. This is where TESSs are often at their most effective, working with other agencies to support the whole family so that poverty, homelessness, poor accommodation and poor health can be tackled to prevent these becoming a barrier to effective education. Children cannot be educated in isolation from these issues.

Many people in our society see Gypsy and Traveller families as dysfunctional and anti-social and this is a view that we often see aired in the press and wider media. Families are often judged to be negligent for failing to send their children to school. Little thought is given to the previous history of the family, which may have been one of constant eviction or sending their children to school only to find that they are bullied and

victimised there. Another sign of perceived dysfunctional behaviour is inconsistent attendance. This is sometimes seen as a sign of chaotic and unpredictable behaviour, when it can actually be a sign of the parents' caring deeply for the children and nursing them through minor illnesses or caring for other relatives in the extended family as well as travelling in order to work.

Through working collaboratively with families the wider issues facing them can be addressed and trusting relationships can be established; the children can see that everyone is working together for their benefit. The nature of the relationship is important and should not be based on dependency, but rather seek to empower the families to take responsibility and have a degree of control over their lives. This requires that time is taken to understand and respect the views and cultural beliefs of the families and to develop responses that offer realistic solutions. Schools will need to be flexible, to be Willows rather than Oaks and to ensure that the extended schools programme has something to offer all children.

Children who are confident that they are safe, secure and valued members of both the school and the wider community are better prepared to fully participate and contribute to school and community life.

Who is going to hold this work together? Who can support the family, signpost to and collaborate with other services and agencies, advise colleagues in school and have oversight of the educational development of these highly marginalised communities? At present this work is undertaken by TESSs, but who will do it and how can it be managed if all services become fully integrated and locality based?

Holding the baton
(ensuring stability and continuity)

Narrowing the Gap recognises that "vulnerable children generally face more disruption in their lives than other children". Ensuring stability and continuity is quite a challenge for mobile and semi-settled communities. Even settled Gypsy Roma Traveller communities face discrimination, marginalisation and racial abuse if their ethnicity is known. Everyone in education recognises that stability and continuity are necessary pre-requisites for progression. Most educational planning is made on the presumption that children will stay in one school for each phase of their education.

Over the years the DCSF has worked with TESSs to

---

[34] Derrington, C. and Kendall, S. (2004). Gypsy Traveller Students in Secondary Schools: Culture, Identity and Achievement. Stoke on Trent: Trentham Books. This study uses the metaphor of 'oaks' and 'willows' to describe the ethos and inclusive practices of secondary schools. 'Oak' schools were rigid and unyielding in their application of policies whereas 'willow' schools accepted the need to respond more flexibly to individual needs.

put in place systems to facilitate pupil records transfer systems for Gypsy Roma and Traveller pupils moving between local authorities, but these have not been sufficiently effective to warrant ongoing funding. TESSs and schools have made careful arrangements to ensure effective transitions at each phase. At secondary level, and to some extent at primary, TESSs expend a great deal of time and energy trying to keep Gypsy Roma and Traveller students engaged with education. Many schools do go the extra mile to provide an appropriate curriculum, but sometimes, where there are behaviour and attendance issues, schools will not follow up when students stop attending. In some cases parents may mislead schools, saying for instance, that they have gone to stay with a relative in another part of the country or even in a different country. Gypsy and Traveller families have discovered that they are far less likely to be prosecuted for non-attendance if their children are not on a school roll, so transitions can be times when children drop out of the system. The experience and knowledge of families that most TESSs possess enable them to support transitions and challenge families who take the opportunity to disengage their children.

A significant number of families live in a different LA from the one in which their children go to school, and cross-borough liaison is an area for improvement in many authorities. Close monitoring is necessary to ensure that educational arrangements do not break down and result in children being lost to the education system.

Distance and learning are other techniques that TESSs have developed to promote continuity of learning for mobile children. (See the section on Distance Learning)

Just as in a relay race, it is important to hold on to the baton for Traveller pupils, to move forward swiftly, and to pass it securely to the next person when the time comes. Whatever the system for provision within a local authority, it needs to ensure that responsibility is not so widely distributed that Gypsy Roma Traveller children can be lost to education. This is probably the most important function carried out by TESSs at present, and in the move to more integrated working recommended by Every Child Matters and Narrowing the Gap it should be carefully nurtured.

Learning to Learn

This section of the document talks about creating a secure learning environment where teaching and learning are personalised to the individual and build on each child's strength. The importance of early intervention is stressed, as are the skills of listening, perseverance, negotiation and problem solving.

"Since we cannot know what knowledge will be most needed in the future, it is senseless to try to teach it in advance. Instead, we should try to turn out people who love learning so much and learn so well that they will be able to learn whatever needs to be learned."[35]

Gypsy Roma Traveller families educate their children. They tell stories about their family history and they love to pass on the stories attached to treasured family photographs. The culture is an oral one and an active one. Boys and girls learn the skills that they will need in order to function well as a member of a Traveller community. No matter which community they come from, they will be learning how to operate within it both economically and socially. For example, Fairground or Show children will see their fathers and mothers booking the fairs; they will see the rides being renovated and the paintwork being refreshed in the winter and they will probably help their families within the scope of their ability. They will see the business being conducted from their homes, they will know about paying the casual workforce, keeping records for VAT, marketing and publicity. Often, by the age of 14 or 15, they will own a small business which they are learning to operate themselves. Their learning relates directly to their way of life and economic sustainability.

This practical learning is common to all the groups. We have seen teachers in school astounded by watching a Romani girl with Special Educational Needs making a beautiful Christmas holly wreath. We have been told stories about the huge fund of knowledge that New Traveller children have about the natural world and edible plants. A twelve year-old Irish Traveller girl who had just entered school for the first time and was perceived to be extremely needy came into her own when, on an activity day, she was part of a group asked to design and build a bridge. At first she stood back and watched proceedings, then she came forward with her suggestions and began to organise the group; in the end, this group won first prize for the structure and the child who had been perceived to be the weakest showed her strength. Roma children learn to play musical instruments and dance from an early age, and in a similar way, can astonish their classmates with high levels of skill acquired outside the school setting.

It is clear that families with limited experience of school-based learning are nevertheless able to provide effective learning experiences for their children, drawing on practical learning, relevance and purpose. The TESS will encourage schools to recognise such community-based education, and perhaps allow the methods used to influence mainstream practice. All children need to feel physically and emotionally secure, they need to be resilient, stimulated, engaged and able to communicate in order to learn.

Just as TESSs encourage schools to see the purpose of the learning that takes place at home, it is important

[35] John Holt, How Children Learn, 1967.

that families come to understand the value of what they are learning in school. Children need to have some control over their own learning and to be able to identify the ways in which newly acquired literacy and numeracy skills can be of use in their own lives.

It is not unusual for pupils to commence their education later than others. If children are first admitted to school in the middle years of primary or even in the secondary years, then the fact that they cannot read or write does not automatically mean that they have learning difficulties. Their need is to be introduced to the new skills for the first time just as other, albeit younger, children are. For these children 'early intervention' means getting on with putting an appropriate personalised learning programme in place, rather than waiting for specialist intervention from, for example, an Educational Psychologist. Time spent in school is precious as we don't know how long it will be sustained, and the child needs to feel that the time spent there is stimulating and productive. Each school plays an important role in the child's life as it forms an important part of their view about the value and enjoyment of learning. Traveller children will benefit from opportunities to catch up with their peers but, most importantly, the children need to feel that they have made progress and contributed positively to the life of the school.

There is a Chinese proverb "A child's life is like a piece of paper on which every passer-by leaves a mark". This is so true for Gypsy Roma Traveller children, who are likely to mix with more "settled people" in their school years than at any other point in their lives. The trusting relationships we foster and the growth in self-esteem we facilitate, will create a lasting impression of both school and "the settled community" that will stay with children forever.

In 2003 an HMI report observed:
"Few of the Gypsy, Roma and Traveller pupils currently in school have had the opportunity to attend any form of pre-school or early years setting." [36]

Despite the fact that this was written some years ago, it is still true in many areas and more recent work on Gypsy Roma Traveller Inclusion in early years settings by Save the Children came to the same conclusion.[37] There can be a variety of reasons for this. Some of them are practical and are to do with the levels of attendance required by pre-schools that can preclude travelling. Other reasons are that parents feel that three years old is too early to leave the family and that the children are too young to have to deal with any possible prejudice they may meet. Many parents do not feel that they want to expose their children to non-gypsy culture at such an early age and others are concerned about leaving their young children with strangers.

In order to alleviate these difficulties, outreach work can increase the confidence of Gypsy Roma

Traveller communities in both early years staff and in the provision itself. All early years workers should receive effective training to support them in their work, to ensure that they have the knowledge and skills to include Gypsy Roma Travellers in early years settings and the understanding to enable them to be sensitive to the home culture.

Settings will need to be in a position to reflect home culture in a way that builds on the first hand experience of the child by, for example, having a home corner that is like a caravan for some of the time; having books and stories that include images of Travelling children or posters and displays that reflect Gypsy Roma Traveller children's experiences.

Cornflakes to canoeing

Narrowing the Gap recommends that extended schooling should have a particular emphasis on socio-economic disadvantage. Once again, the document stresses the importance of multiple providers working together to provide a comprehensive 'core offer' giving disadvantaged children opportunities they might otherwise miss.

Achieving success in this strand may present significant challenges when working with Gypsy Roma Traveller communities. Families can be very suspicious of unnecessary contact with Gorja (settled) communities, fearing that children may lose their home culture, especially through the mixing of teenage boys and girls. Families have deeply held beliefs about care of children. Their culture holds that nobody can care for children better than their parents and they are very uncertain about trusting their care to people outside the family. Interestingly, for a group of people that is often collectively known as "Travellers" by the mainstream community, families can be really troubled by transport difficulties. Many families rely on school transport because the family vehicle is often the one the father uses for his work. Even if it is available at the beginning of the day, it may not be available at the end of the school day as it will still be in working use. For children dependent on school transport, early starts for breakfast and late finishes for wider activities present difficulties if the school transport is not available to support the journey to and from school.

Extended schooling offers huge possibilities to Gypsy Roma Traveller communities; there are greater opportunities for 'catch-up' classes, opportunities to learn basic and wider skills, massive opportunities for

[36] DCSF Aiming High: Raising the achievement of Gypsy and Traveller Pupils – A guide to good practice. 2003.

[37] Save the Children UK. Early Years Outreach Practice Guide. 2007.

enhancement through the development of music, arts and sport. This more flexible time offers opportunities to engage in activities that support the Community Cohesion agenda. There are opportunities for Gypsy Roma Travellers and settled people to work together to discover their similarities and celebrate their (really very small) differences. After this work is in place we may be able to live in a world where Gypsy Roma Traveller families can find a place to live without a massive public outcry.

Research[38] for the National Evaluation of the Children's Fund looked at a project aimed at engaging Gypsy Roma Traveller children in out-of-school leisure activities. It found that attempts to ensure the project became self-sufficient and continued beyond the end of the funded period were hampered by the following:
• income levels and the cost of leisure activities;

• mothers' wish for respite, which was at odds with the policy of seeking actively to engage parents in service provision;

• lack of spare time available for mothers;

• lack of suitable and accessible transport;

• lack of basic skills (such as literacy);

• family priorities (eg, for the father's use of the car for work).

This gives some indication of the issues that will need to be taken into consideration if the Extended School service is to reach out to Gypsy Roma Traveller communities.

It will be a long journey to learn the needs of Gypsy Roma Traveller local communities and to design a programme of extended activities to meet their needs, then to build trust and empathy, but it is worth undertaking to ensure that Britain's most marginalised communities are given a place in our society alongside all other communities.

Unite to succeed
(Multi-agency working)

The subtitle of this section of Narrowing the Gap, 'Sanity not Vanity', gives pause for thought. If a vanity exists within TESSs it is probably one that says they can do this work better than anyone else. This is not surprising, because there is scant evidence that others have shown great interest in the work in the past. Twenty-five years or more ago TESSs were told that schools had an open door policy and those working in Traveller Education

at that time found that although the doors were open, the Gypsy Roma Traveller pupils were not going through them and the reasons for this are well-documented throughout this book.

Over the years TESSs moved away from separate provision, through bridging to school, into mainstream primary and then into SEN departments in secondary education and finally through differentiation and into inclusion. TESSs were pushing the door further open at every stage and discovering wider needs within the family, for accommodation and access to all of the public services.

In school there were issues about access to the curriculum, resources and materials that reflected Gypsy Roma Traveller culture, as well as suitability and access to skills-based learning in the Secondary phase. In the community there were issues of poverty, discrimination, poor accommodation or, worse, no access to accommodation, poor access to health services, social services, adult learning and careers advice. TESS rolled their sleeves up and got on with this work. They really know how to knock on doors – and that's not just caravan doors. They know how to work with others and work in a bottom–up multi-agency way. At one stage some TESS were like miniature education departments in themselves with teachers, EWOs, transport and school uniform budgets and Connexions workers among those who were attached to Services. For anything to do with Gypsy Roma Travellers the TESS was an early port of call. The intention was mainstreaming, but perhaps it is useful to consider the quotation from Gandhi: "Be the change you want to see in the world". Despite this, there was still a need for multi-agency working. There was also frustration that grass root inter-agency working was rarely recognised or understood at a more strategic level.

Now, however, this strand of Narrowing the Gap requires a different strategy, not bottom-up, but top-down. It demands vision and commitment from the upper levels of the local authority, health and police services to establish priorities and communicate them throughout their teams. This is followed up with "relentless inter-disciplinary training" by an integrated training team, which should include education, social services and the voluntary sector. For Gypsy Roma Travellers we would add community members, TESS staff, health and Gypsy Liaison Officers to the training team so that unity is demonstrated and inter-agency work reinforced. The success of this top-down approach will depend on the extent to which Gypsy Roma Traveller communities and TESS are consulted on the new ways of working, to prevent losing the gains that have already been made in reaching out to Gypsy Roma Traveller communities. The needs of these relatively small and isolated groups will need to be recognised in an authority-wide structure and the existing strengths of specialist services will need to be safeguarded if the gains of the past are to be built upon.

---

[38] Research Report RR734 DCSF, Edwards, A., Barnes, M., Plewis, I. and Morris, K., et al. (2006).

Shape up and keep fit – a well-qualified and adaptable workforce

This thread focuses on developing core skills across the children's workforce, having systems for common assessment – and lead professional roles for driving forward multi-agency work around individual children with identified needs.

Many TESSs are already deeply involved in working in 'team around the child' initiatives and find that the skills of multi-agency working come easily. However, others involved in the Common Assessment Framework may not be accustomed to these working practices and care needs to be taken that these multi-agency meetings do not just become 'talking-shops'. They need to be in a position to ensure that effective action can be taken to engage vulnerable children in suitable provision where they can be properly safeguarded.

The CAF is a key part of delivering frontline services that are integrated and are focused around the needs of children and young people. The CAF is a standardised approach to conducting assessments of children's additional needs and deciding how these should be met. It can be used by practitioners across children's services in England.

The CAF promotes more effective, earlier identification of additional needs, particularly in universal services. It aims to provide a simple process for a holistic assessment of children's needs and strengths, taking account of the roles of parents, carers and environmental factors on their development. Practitioners are then better placed to agree with children and families about appropriate modes of support. The CAF also aims to improve integrated working by promoting coordinated service provisions.

http://www.dcsf.gov.uk/everychildmatters/ strategy/deliveringservices1/caf/cafframework/

This means that the involvement of TESSs in 'team around the child meetings' should mean that their knowledge about culture, identity and mobility are the areas that are of most importance. Also, TESS staff do not necessarily need to be the 'lead professional' if the child is a Gypsy Roma Traveller with a Special Educational Need or disability or if the issue is largely about something unconnected with their ethnicity. Ethnicity, identity and lifestyle will always have an impact on the child and this will be the context of the assessment.

Young Roma women are sometimes "married" in the eyes of their community before they are legally permitted to be. In most cases, the man will be older and in a few cases significantly so. Such cases involve a number of child protection issues and serious criminal offences, so a referral to Social Services must be made in every case. Any relationship has the potential to be abusive, particularly so when there is a significant age gap between the partners and the woman is still a child. Close monitoring is necessary to ensure that abuse is not taking place. Romani culture expects the couple to live together and start a family as soon as possible and, in our experience, most newly "married" Roma share this view, so the safety and well-being of an infant enter into the equation. As with other teenage mothers, pregnancy can disrupt education and opportunities, and the husband may have a say in what his young wife is entitled to do.

The cultural context does, however, need to be made explicit. Most of these relationships are entered into voluntarily, and any pregnancy will be planned and welcomed. The young mother will live with the father, but also with the baby's grandparents, who will provide advice guidance and support for the new mother. This support network could be used to safeguard and promote the well-being of the mother and child. On the other hand, the young mother may welcome the opportunity to make contact with other teenage mothers, to return to school or have access to parenting classes.

We are not aware of prosecutions resulting from such relationships, although sometimes the partners have been expected to live apart until the woman is of age. In most cases, however, a gently supportive regime is put in place to ensure that the young mother knows where to turn if support is needed.

This raises the issue of training and sharing skills. TESSs are small specialist services who well understand the need to deliver training to a wide range of colleagues. They are keen to keep in touch with developments in provision for children. Senior managers will need to have a good understanding of the issues around the education of the Gypsy Roma Traveller communities, as there will need to be decisions about the expectations and outcomes required of the TESSs. Should the service be largely involved in training colleagues in schools and in Children's Services to ensure that the knowledge base is more widely understood? Is the main issue engagement with the community and building trust and confidence in the education system? It would seem that advisory work in schools is of great importance ensuring that colleagues are well informed and have a good knowledge of the learning needs, the culture and lifestyle for the Gypsy Roma Traveller communities.

In the twenty-first century the children's workforce is required to be multi-skilled. An important aspect of the required skill sets is a confident understanding of the complex issues around equality and diversity.

For more on this topic see the next chapter.

Prove it - making change happen

This section of Narrowing the Gap addresses information-sharing across and between services, the voice of the child and the family and appropriate performance indicators.

Setting performance indicators is a strong theme running through Narrowing the Gap, but setting targets for Gypsy Roma Traveller children and communities is very challenging. (These issues are discussed in the chapter on Judging Success). Widespread distrust of the settled community with its institutions, its databases, targets and inflexibility in understanding and accepting Gypsy Roma Traveller culture and way of life have inevitably led many in these communities to be suspicious of the settled community and all that it represents.

For TESSs a primary target is building good trusting relationships with the community that will support access to education. The Gypsy Roma Travellers want access to education, but not if the cost to their children's happiness is too great. Nor do they wish to become assimilated and lose a culture of which they are very proud.

This requires excellent communication and understanding of the views of parents and children. Personalisation is on the agenda for all children and in every school. For Gypsy Roma Traveller pupils who may miss education through mobility or join school late this will offer additional strategies and solutions.

Services want children to achieve success in school, but recognise that admitting Gypsy Roma Traveller children to school can have a detrimental effect on school attendance and results, at least at first. The National Strategies have recognised that Gypsy Roma Traveller children's attainment is so low that it will take many decades at current levels of achievement for children to reach national performance averages.

The targets we set will still need to be focused on engagement with the education system. Significant numbers of Gypsy Roma Traveller children move between schools and authorities in the course of a Key Stage, so raw SATs scores and even contextual value-added measures will not indicate how effective provision has been in meeting their needs. Data collection will often need to be in the form of tracking pupil progress, as numbers in a cohort can be very low and rarely meet the criteria for statistical significance.

Tracking data needs to be read in the context of information about mobility and access to education. Tracking data needs to transfer with pupils to ensure that the maximum benefit is derived from time in school, and the disruptive effects of mobility minimised.

For more on success criteria and performance indicators see the section in "Judging Success", the next chapter.

From good to great - effective joint commissioning of Children's Services

The move to joint planning and commissioning across local authority services offers many opportunities for a step forward in the effective delivery of services to Gypsy Roma Traveller communities. The vision for the future is that joint planning and commissioning will lead to the needs of this vulnerable group being assessed and more widely understood. New priorities will be set and the workforce will have an agreed vision for delivering quality services. Integrated working will mean that the provision for vulnerable children will improve and there will be fewer gaps in it.

TESSs, accustomed to multi-agency working, will welcome these developments and wish to contribute their experience and expertise to them. However, there are concerns that the structures should support and develop the good practice that has been developed over the years. We have seen that there is a need for Gypsy Roma Traveller communities to receive multi-agency support and that there are many ways of achieving this.

Having an identified TESS is not the only way of supporting the inclusion, achievement and opportunities of Gypsy Roma Traveller pupils, but if there were no TESS there would need to be a significant redistribution of responsibilities within the LA to ensure that the services currently offered were covered. Gypsy Roma Travellers are very demanding of time and energy, and the measurable outcomes are not always impressive; for example, the number of interactions necessary to prevent a young person disengaging will almost certainly be greater than for most other groups. There is a real danger that, if responsibilities were transferred to colleagues with more general roles, challenging Gypsy Roma Traveller learners would not receive the level of support necessary to enable them to reach their full potential.

There are a number of LAs which do not have TESS and it is clear that no alternative support mechanisms have emerged; families moving into these areas frequently contact the TESS in the area they have left, and referrals made to the welcoming LA rarely result in appropriate responses.

The skills of building trusting relationships with Gypsy Roma Traveller communities whom others characterise as 'hard to reach' are well developed in TESSs, and the capacity to be both supportive and demanding is a defining feature of workers in this area. Traveller services have developed skills in early intervention, though it can mean something very different to them. For most of the LA, early intervention happens as part of Early Years Education, but for TESS early intervention commences the first time there is an interaction with a family and a child, even if that child is 14 years old. In other words, LAs have much to gain from considering the TESSs very rounded view of the needs and achievements of vulnerable pupils. LAs may be interested in monitoring how effective their mainstream services are in identifying and responding to the needs of vulnerable and hard to reach communities; but they might also consider retaining dedicated support for Traveller Education, to act as a safety net and ensure that their safeguarding duty is functioning well for Gypsy Roma Traveller Children

The unique functions of TESSs, which would need to be safeguarded under any mainstreaming agenda, include:
- Work in partnership with schools and other agencies to deliver the full ECM agenda
- Monitoring mainstream service delivery and acting as a safety net where families fall through the net
- Participation in a national network to support educational continuity for mobile learners (including Distance Learning Support)
- Work with colleagues in adjacent TESSs to provide effective support for families accessing services across LA boundaries
- Provision of activities and resources to support an affirming curriculum and events, such as Gypsy Roma Traveller History Month
- Provision of CPD for school and LA staffs to build capacity and to mainstream provision
- Provision of consultancy information and advice to schools to achieve the best outcomes for schools and families
- Provision of advice to enable Gypsy Roma Traveller families to become independent users of the education system.

Alignment of education support for Gypsy Roma Travellers

Traveller participation in mainstream education

In January 2003 the nature of Traveller Education changed irrevocably. The change came as a result of the introduction of two new ethnic codes for Gypsy Roma (WROM) and Traveller of Irish Heritage (WIRT) on school admission forms and in the school census returns. The data was incomplete and unreliable, but the story it told was shocking and could not be ignored.

- Declining participation rates at secondary school; only a third of the number of Gypsy Roma pupils and less than half of Travellers of Irish Heritage were recorded at Key Stage 4 compared to Key Stage 1.

- Gypsy Roma and Travellers of Irish Heritage pupils had very low attainment throughout Key Stage assessments and also have much higher identification of special educational needs.

- Higher percentages of Gypsy Roma and Travellers of Irish Heritage pupils attended Special Schools than any other group.

- Travellers of Irish Heritage were the ethnic group most likely to be permanently excluded, with a rate nearly four times that of the average for all pupils. Gypsy Roma also had higher rates of permanent exclusion.

There have been powerful reports in the past - the Ofsted report Raising the achievement of Minority Ethnic pupils, the Aiming High reports and HMI reports - highlighting the issues of Gypsy Roma Traveller underachievement, but it is in their nature that they begin to go out-of-date and be forgotten from the day they are published. Data, on the other hand, are regularly refreshed, with one set reviving interest in previous ones; is there an improving trend?

The achievement of Gypsy Roma Travellers became a national priority, with increasing references in policy documents and incorporation into the National Strategies. At Local Authority level "The New Relationship with Schools" redefined the role of centrally-employed staff, working increasingly on a consultancy model where schools monitor their own provision, establish their need for support and the School Improvement Partner brokers in appropriate support.

Traveller Education Services had developed a way of working which met the needs of families and schools. They took every opportunity they got to deliver training and build capacity, but before 2003 there was little interest at local authority level. Services were allowed to get on with their jobs but rarely had an impact on policy development and planning. TESSs often wrote themselves into Education Development Plans only to find they disappeared again when a new version was published. The introduction of the ethnic codes came as a result of lobbying by professional and voluntary organisations and significant documents like Aiming High: Raising the Attainment of Gypsy Traveller Pupils and The Inclusion of Gypsy, Roma and Traveller Children and Young People represented strategic collaboration between central government and Traveller Education professionals. TESS staff joined the National Strategies as Regional Advisers and the Strategies began to organise regional meetings to synchronise the work of TESS with broader initiatives.

The DCSF retains a commitment to Traveller education support, funding Gypsy Roma Traveller History Month, national research and distance learning initiatives. It recognises the value of the national network of TESSs, has a close working relationship with NATT+ and has supported the publication and promotion of culturally appropriate resources. From 2010 Local Authorities are expected to set Key Stage 2 and Key Stage 4 targets for combined Gypsy Roma and Travellers of Irish Heritage cohorts.

Local difficulties

At local authority level the picture is somewhat different. In a number of authorities TESSs are losing staff and in some cases losing their identity as a separate service. The mainstreaming changes outlined above, which had been generally sought and welcomed by Traveller Education professionals, coincided with a change in the basis of funding, and was itself part of a major shift in government policy relating to the reduction of bureaucracy and changes in monitoring systems. Between 1989 and 2003 funding for Traveller Education was ring-fenced as a separate grant, then as part of the Ethnic Minority Achievement grant and finally within the Standards fund. From April 2003 the ring-fence was extended when the Vulnerable Children Grant merged several Standards Fund Grants, including the Traveller Achievement Grant, and made available £84 million - a substantial increase on the grants it replaced which totalled £31 million in 2002. The VCG grant allowed LAs to allocate funding based on local needs in order to provide support to a range of vulnerable children, including those from Gypsy and Traveller backgrounds.

In 2008 the Vulnerable Children's Grant (and hence the funding for Traveller Education Support) was incorporated into the Area Based Grant. The purpose is summed up as follows.

Government has significantly increased local authorities' flexibility over the use of their mainstream resources by moving over £4bn of grants into the new non-ring-fenced Area Based Grant (ABG). This will minimise the barriers to local authorities using their mainstream resources to support local priorities where they wish to do so.

The grant covers a very wide range of local authority functions and, to be blunt, support for Traveller Education is a very low priority indeed. In practice, the very large pot of money is haggled over and divided between departments, divisions, services and teams in a way which rarely presents opportunities for making the case for developing the work to meet new challenges. Some services no longer have their own budgets, and when staff leave or retire, there is a reluctance to replace them. This isn't strategic planning, but finance-driven pragmatism, which is undermining the effectiveness and morale of services locally and nationally.

Although the amount of Area Based Grant available has been increased, the requirement for authorities to match-fund grant aid has been removed; so, if authorities choose to regard their previous contribution as a potential saving, then pressure on the grant will grow. This is the situation as we enter a period when there are likely to be public sector cuts so the prospects for Traveller Education support look very bleak indeed.

In its report Gypsies and Travellers: Simple solutions for living together, the Equalities and Human Rights Commission reviewed progress made since 'Common Ground' was published by Commission for Racial Equality in 2006. One of its recommendations is that the DCSF undertake a review of Traveller Education Support Services.

In this context we want to consider how Traveller Education professionals should function within a mainstream service. In the next five sections, we summarise the key tasks that, we believe, need to be undertaken to ensure the inclusion and opportunities of children and young people from these communities. The core principle should be that, if a mainstream service can do the job well, it should do so. The extent to which these functions can be mainstreamed will depend on the structures and organisation of LA services. Where there is a Traveller Education Service, it may not be reasonable or recommended for it to undertake all these functions; a proper assessment of the staffing levels and the range of needs should be undertaken to create conditions under which it is possible for staff to do a good job.

Building capacity among families and community

1) Using a variety of links (including community and family, schools, other agencies and TESSs) to identify all Gypsy Roma Traveller families living in and visiting the authority,
   a) establish their needs and their capacity to access education
   b) provide the information and advice they need to access education
   c) monitor access and inclusion.

2) Dialogue with families to promote understanding of the education system:
   a) benefits of pre-school access
   b) parental support for learning
   c) how to raise concerns
   d) phase transfer options
   e) Key Stage 4 and 5 opportunities.

3) Monitor and support independent access, inclusion and continuity:
   a) approach all families with early years children
   b) approach all families with rising 5 children
   c) support for phase transfer
   d) encourage engagement and prevent exclusion at Key Stages 3 and 4
   e) support choices at Key Stage 4 and beyond.

4) Support for parental and community participation in school and LA:
   a) create opportunities for volunteering and employment of Gypsy Roma Travellers
   b) liaise with the community around their participation in Gypsy Roma Traveller History Month events, training and resource production.

Building capacity within the LA

a) Monitor Gypsy Roma Traveller children and young people, from birth to 19 (especially those out of school, with poor attendance, highly mobile and Not in Education Employment and Training)

b) Information sharing with Research and Statistics to develop accurate LA profile of Gypsy Roma Traveller Learners, including pupils not ascribing to the WIRT and WROM categories:
   i. identify all Gypsy Roma Traveller families
   ii. monitor arrivals, departures and moves within LA
   iii. liaise with other TESSs to support continuity
   iv. identify and try to trace missing children and children missing education

c) Contribute to training (Newly Qualified Teachers, Teaching Assistants, Ethnic Minority Achievement Coordinators, Strategies)

d) School Improvement Partner liaison and training

e) Partnership on initiatives with identified focus on or benefit to Gypsy Roma Traveller communities

f) Contribution to development of policies impacting on Gypsy Roma Traveller education and well-being (eg, community cohesion, admissions, attendance)

g) Participation in inter-agency working within children's services, the LA and with the voluntary sector

h) Contribution to the development and implementation of good practice at national regional and local level.

Building capacity within schools

a) Participation in LA's support for schools (eg, training, moderation)

b) Encouraging partnerships between schools, Gypsy Roma Traveller communities and families

c) Partnership teaching, planning and consultancy interventions to support inclusive, differentiated practice

d) Identifying resources and materials to support an inclusive and affirming curriculum

e) Support for parental participation and engagement.

Safety net

Alignment and mainstreaming assume that, as far as is practically possible, mainstream provision, inclusive, high-achieving schools backed by a challenging yet supportive LA, should be able to engage with Gypsy Roma Traveller families and respond to their educational needs and entitlements. There is much evidence that this is the case with the growing number of Gypsy Roma Traveller families who have had positive experiences and are committed to supporting their children's access and opportunities.

Not all families fall into this category, often for reasons beyond their control. Schools and local authorities have multiple objectives, and the needs of more marginal families may be overlooked and over-ridden. This is particularly true when families are mobile, in insecure accommodation, under threat or suffering social, economic or psychological distress.

The decision to appoint virtual headteachers to co-ordinate the educational entitlement of Looked After

Children appears to us to mirror the work done by TESSs. There are two differences, however:
1) LAs have statutory responsibilities as a corporate parent
2) Most Looked After Children have a significant number or other professionals engaged with them, while for Gypsy Roma Travellers the TESS is frequently the first and last call.

While it is appropriate that the LA should, as a corporate parent, be expected to take all necessary steps to ensure children are able to access and benefit from education, it is reasonable that Gypsy Roma Travellers who are also vulnerable should be entitled to the same support on Human Rights grounds. Withdrawing Traveller Education support could have a disproportionate impact where that support is the only bridge intact to promote inclusion.

Safeguarding

TESSs perform an important function by ensuring that the local authority's responsibility to safeguard children is effective for Gypsy Roma Traveller families. TESSs are in touch with these communities which many other services find "hard to reach". They are working to find school places for children, prevent exclusions, reduce disaffection and prevent disengagement from education, all of which support the objective of preventing Children Missing Education and thus safeguarding children and young people.

The guidance on "Working together to Safeguard Children"[44] is particularly strong on issues of Equality and diversity it states that:

"Ensuring equality of opportunity
Equality of opportunity means that all children have the opportunity to achieve the best possible development, regardless of their gender, ability, race, ethnicity, circumstances or age. Some vulnerable children may have been particularly disadvantaged in their access to important opportunities, and their health and educational needs will require particular attention in order to optimise their current welfare as well as their long-term outcomes in young adulthood."

This document makes clear the need for all agencies to work together and gives us the following definition of Safeguarding:
• Protecting children and young people from maltreatment

• Preventing the impairment of children and young people's health and development

• Ensuring that children and young people are growing up in circumstances consistent with the provision of safe and effective care

[44] DCSF (2006) Working together to Safeguard Children: A guide to inter-agency working to safeguard and promote the welfare of children on-line at http://www.everychildmatters.gov.uk/resources-and-practice/IG00060/

- Undertaking the role so as to enable those children and young people to have optimum life chances and to enter adulthood successfully.

For Traveller families living on unauthorised encampments, where mobility levels are high, or on marginalised inner city sites where work opportunities are limited, safeguarding can be crucial. The mobility of these groups, with historically poor access to education and training and low levels of functional literacy in the community, needs to be considered seriously within the safeguarding agenda. The issue of under-age Roma marriage and the safeguarding issues involved have been mentioned elsewhere in this book. As with all communities, particularly those under stress, there is domestic violence, which impacts on children in many ways. The reticence of the communities about contacting authority highlights the importance of professionals maintaining regular contact with such families.

TESSs work by establishing a relationship of trust with families, through respect for their identity and support for their right to their way of life. We also have a commitment to education and opportunities which families respect. This relationship is not time limited and we never close a case; where things appear to be working well we maintain a watching brief. We monitor the engagement and progress of every Gypsy Roma Traveller child we know of in our area between the ages of 0 and 19, intervening where necessary to keep their education on track. We frequently work with overlapping generations so our engagement is seamless. We signpost other agencies and introduce their workers to the families. We also keep visit records which can be important evidence should proceedings start.

In general Gypsy Roma Travellers are less wary of teachers than of social workers. Children are the heart of the families, and professionals who have the power to take them away are feared. Bad experiences have passed into folklore and the suspicion persists. Individual families have good relationships with social workers (particularly those in the voluntary sector such as Family Service Units) but these experiences tend not to change the stereotype.

In the current round of Safeguarding inspections there are certain 'limiting judgements' which prevent the award of a good overall grade and these are:
- Overall effectiveness is likely to be inadequate if either of the two safeguarding outcomes (children and young people are safe and children and young people feel safe) is judged as inadequate

- Overall effectiveness is unlikely to be good or better if either of the two safeguarding outcomes (children and young people are safe and children and young people feel safe) is not judged as good

- Leadership and management are unlikely to be adequate if the grade awarded for equality and diversity is inadequate.

Relationships between TESSs and Safeguarding teams have improved through the development of Children's Services but there is still some way to go. Our approaches are different, but clarity and understanding can be developed through partnership working and casework.

Metaphorical conclusion

Traveller Education is like a local transport network with local buses and trains, picking up families and children from a range of locations and delivering them to various points in the education system. This network is friendly, patient and responsive to local needs.

The mainline service operators have never been concerned to fit in with our timetables and connections; it has been up to us to design our services to fit in with them. They have mainline targets and they won't wait for anyone. But there has been growing concern that some people have been losing out so they've laid on a special train, picking up at two new stations WIRT and WROM going direct to Achievement at Key Stage 4. Which is great if you make the connection. The problem is, if you aren't in the right place at the right time, or if for some reason you need to stop off en route, you can be stranded. In that case you're back to the local network which will help you reconnect at some other point. You may be delayed, but we'll get you there in the end. The mainline service is important but it doesn't replace the local network; it needs to be integrated with it.

Pause for thought

1) To what extent are mainstream services equipped and motivated to address the educational needs of Gypsy Roma Traveller families?

2) As a TESS could you do any more to build the capacity of families, schools and the LA? If you could, what is standing in your way?

3) As an LA do you think your TESS has gone native? If it has, why do you think it happened, and what have you done about it?

4) As a family, is it important for TESSs to survive or have they done their job?

5) As a school, what do you think is the appropriate role for a TESS to take?

6) As a local authority, which of the tasks above could be absorbed into Integrated Services and where does the specialist expertise of your TESS reside? How can you ensure that the LA has wider ownership of the issues of Traveller education whilst preserving the gains that have been made by your existing service?

Managing support for the education of Gypsy Roma Travellers

Management models

Traveller Education Support Services are managed in many different ways. In some authorities, they are part of the Ethnic Minority Achievement Service, which itself may have been subsumed into a school improvement service. In others the TESS may be part of the Admissions and Inclusion Service, or Pupil Support. In some areas TESSs no longer have distinct identities. Learning and Teaching Consultants for Gypsy Roma Traveller pupils (or even for a wider group such as vulnerable children) may be located within the National Strategies teams and Inclusion officers within a Welfare and Inclusion Service. Some authorities are members of a consortium and receive Traveller Education support from a lead borough employing and managing staff on their behalf.

Managing child and family focused services

Wherever the TESS is located, there is a good chance it won't fit comfortably into the management structure. This is due mainly to the breadth of the remit of Traveller Education support; it covers the age range from birth to 19, works across the curriculum and with a broad range of professional and agencies across the Every Child Matters agenda. This illustrates the range of partnerships that need to be maintained to ensure every child is able to meet his or her full potential.

Most responsibilities within LAs tend to focus around a single element of the educational process such as admissions, curriculum or standards, rather than the whole education of particular groups of children. There are exceptions, and these are instructive. Virtual headteachers oversee the educational engagement and well-being of Looked After Children, while other staff work with specific groups, such as refugees and asylum seekers and teenage parents. What these groups have in common is their vulnerability, complex needs and the danger of their becoming disengaged from the education system.

In the two examples below we can see how some aspects of the role harmonise with the work of the managing department, while other aspects are out of tune with patterns of working.

If the TESS is part of an inclusion service, managers will understand the pupil and family focused approach to the work. Colleagues in these departments are likely to be familiar with and support the inter-agency role of Traveller Education professionals, as will school staff who have to work in the same way with vulnerable and SEN pupils. But an inclusion-focused management will have less capacity to support many of the school-focused interventions around the curriculum and pupil progress that TESSs undertake. There can also be tensions around core functions; the role adopted by most TESSs as the friend and advocate to Gypsy Roma Traveller families may be at odds with target-driven enforcement approaches to non-attendance.

Where Traveller Education support is located within a School Improvement Service there is plenty of potential for partnership working around National Strategies Initiatives and the provision of teaching and learning consultancy support to schools around the curriculum, community cohesion and staff development. Managers in these settings find it more difficult to take on board the responsibilities to those children and young people who are between schools, and families who are grappling with a range of issues that are undermining their children's capacity to learn.

The New Relationship with schools

Achievement remains the yardstick against which all interventions are assessed, by Ofsted, the National Strategies and LAs. While there is increasing recognition of the "long tail of under-achievement" and a renewed focus on narrowing the gap, reaching level 4 and 5 at Key Stage 2 and five or more A*-C at GCSE (including English and Maths) is the target of most of the strands. Although Contextual Value Added is increasingly used to monitor progress, the emphasis on "narrowing the gap" reminds us that reaching the expected level is still the outcome that matters.

Data and statistics are the drivers of school improvement, used by School Improvement Partners and Ofsted to identify the strengths and weaknesses of schools. The aim, to reduce to a minimum the number of children failing to reach national expectations and to increase the proportion exceeding those expectations, certainly contributes to improving the quality of teaching and learning. Gypsy Roma Traveller pupils do better in good schools, and the more good schools there are, the better they will do. But unfortunately the data-driven approach has limited value in responding to the sometimes complex needs of individual Gypsy Roma Traveller pupils, particularly those whose engagement with schools is disrupted or undermined by a range of issues across the Every Child Matters agenda.

The New Relationship with schools in many ways clarified and simplified the relationship between schools and LAs. The services of centrally employed staff are brokered in by the school, in consultation with the School Improvement Partner, to respond to strategic development needs identified through an analysis of data. Where the numbers of Gypsy Roma Travellers in a school is small, where they have not been identified and where the school faces more pressing challenges, the New Relationship with schools may not prioritise the needs of these groups. Conversely the TESS may need to intervene quickly in response to a crisis, a referral from a family or other agency, or mobility issues. The New Relationship with schools contributes to strategic development, but the old relationship needs to be maintained to ensure these children remain engaged and achieve their full entitlement. Schools are accustomed to working in inter-agency, child- and family-focused ways, but LAs are less comfortable with their staff adopting the same approach.

The role TESSs have taken over the years is similar to that developed quite recently to respond to the needs of Looked After Children. There is a recognition that although a wide range of professionals and carers may be involved with any particular Looked After Child, there is a need for a single person to ensure that all the interventions dovetail. The role of the TESSs is similar, trying to put children onto the educational track, and keep them there until they reach adulthood. The educational track might include Children's Centres, Pupil Referral Units, Alternative Education Providers, Distance Learning, Colleges and Family Education. TESSs don't really work on a basis of percentages, neither do they ever close a case. As a child settles into school, the TESS will withdraw to a monitoring and consultancy role, but will remain available to the family and the school should something happen in school or outside which causes education to break down. The aim is to enable every child with whom they are in contact to maintain continuity of education and thereby reach their full potential.

Being strategic

There needs to be a balance between strategic developmental work and responsive work. Strategic interventions contribute to long-term change, but responsive interventions are frequently necessary to keep the show on the road and to deal with short-term change. Change characterises the lives of many families, so there is a danger that responsiveness may take priority over development. Families and schools expect a response to their phone calls and messages, and most TESS staff get satisfaction from being efficient in this respect. But sometimes these immediate demands are symptoms rather than

causes, and the causes may be treated better by strategic responses. TESSs frequently play a mediating role between families and schools, setting up and participating in meetings, necessary because there is a degree of apprehension on both sides, born of a mutual lack of familiarity and understanding. A strategic approach would be to build awareness and understanding between families and schools so that effective communication is established as a matter of course, encouraging schools and parents to engage in dialogue from the outset, with the TESS troubleshooting only if necessary.

Not only is it necessary to work in both ways, but each approach can contain elements of the other. Strategic interventions may be supported by a reactive safety net, such as an encouraging phone call (or visit) before a family visit a school independently and a follow-up afterwards. Reactive interventions can be used to develop strategic partnerships; a school visit to discuss a specific problem may be steered into a broader discussion about ethos and awareness.

Strategic development and responses to rapidly changing day-to-day demands of schools and families need to be balanced. School improvement tends to be strategic, seeking over time to improve the quality of provision through development plans based on national and local priorities, delivered down the line so that personal targets will ultimately contribute to national targets, leading to a steady improvement "across the piece." The Gypsy Roma Traveller Achievement Programme, the History Month, National Gypsy Roma Traveller resource lists and E-lamp are all examples of a Gypsy Roma Traveller perspective being fed into National policies, and the message is now coming down the line "and what are we doing about Gypsy Roma Travellers?"

This model, however, will not pick up all the educational support needs of Gypsy Roma Traveller communities. They, like Looked After Children and other disadvantaged groups, don't fit easily into the strategic development model. The circumstances they have to deal with and the demands they make change rapidly, and can easily derail their fragile educational engagement. Schools are institutions which achieve a great deal with a broad range of children, including many Gypsy Roma Traveller pupils. But most Gypsy Roma Traveller children will have periods when their education loses direction. For some children, usually the most vulnerable, their education only stays on the rails with a great deal of effort from all concerned. If pupils and their parents disengage from education, the school's room for manoeuvre becomes limited and, in practice, they may not have the time and energy to address the multiple issues that might be undermining a child's education. This is not a criticism of schools, just recognition that their resources and flexibility are not infinite. Of course if the problem is school-based or subject to the school's influence, we would expect it to act, but the reasons for educational disengagement may well be complex and beyond the school's sphere of influence.

It is for this reason Traveller Education support must have a child- and family-focused component to it, and consequently line management must be sufficiently informed and flexible to take account of that focus. If the management is through school improvement, there needs to be an acceptance that some staff time and targets will focus on children and families, as well as inter-agency working. Conversely, if the management has a pupil support focus, then there will need to be recognition that Traveller Education staff will need some engagement with school improvement colleagues, to ensure they are up to date and can work collaboratively in areas of benefit to Gypsy Roma Travellers and other vulnerable children.

Now the funding for Traveller Education has become lost within the Area Focused Grant, some managers are inclined to make savings by disbanding their TESSs and assuming that enough has been done for their needs to be met by mainstream provision. Even if responsibility for supporting schools and families in meeting the range of challenges faced by these communities were written into the job descriptions of appropriate professionals, the need for a focused overview would be lost. Even where there is no named TESS there needs to be a forum through which the various professionals supporting families can meet to co-ordinate, review and monitor the effectiveness of their interventions.

Traveller Education grew from the bottom up and practitioners have always had a role in developing policy at a national level. Gradually good practice has been developed and implemented, but the process is dynamic. The levels of attendance and achievement indicate both how far we have come and how far we still have to go.

Joint Commissioning

Joint Commissioning of Services has the potential to overcome many of these issues, as can be seen in the ECM advice on joint commissioning below. BUT the commissioners need to really understand the issues for each group of vulnerable pupils, and consideration must be given to the ways in which the knowledge and understanding of child- and family-centred work that lies within Traveller Education Support Services can be shared with commissioners and other providers within the Children's Trust: *http://www.everychildmatters. gov.uk/strategy/planningandcommissioning/about/*

The documentation gives additional detail about the joint planning and commissioning cycle:
1. Look at the current pattern of outcomes for children and young people in their area, and recent trends, against national and relevant local comparators.

2. Look within the overall picture at outcomes for particular groups of young people.

3. Use all this data, and draw on the views of children, young people and their families, local communities and frontline staff, to develop an overall, integrated needs assessment.

4. Agree on the nature and scale of the local challenge, identify the resources available and set priorities for action.

5. Plan the pattern of service most likely to secure priority outcomes, considering carefully the ways in which resources can be increasingly focused on prevention and early intervention.

6. Decide together how best to purchase or provide (commission) those services, including drawing in alternative providers to widen options and increase efficiency.

7. Develop and extend joint commissioning from pooled budgets and pooled resources.

8. Plan for the workforce development and other changes in local processes and ways of working necessary to support delivery.

9. Monitor and review to ensure services are working to deliver the ambitions set out for them.

This guidance is sufficiently open to enable Local Authorities to plan highly responsive services. However, care needs to be taken in the planning of services for vulnerable minorities. When pupil numbers are low, it can be tempting to amalgamate small services for reasons that are more to do with financial efficiency than carefully considered and effective means of raising achievement for these vulnerable children.

The issues for Gypsy Roma Traveller communities are complex and the working practices developed by Traveller Education Support Services to support inclusive practices and raise attainment have taken many years to evolve. Other inclusion services would have much to learn from the working practices of TESSs. In most cases Traveller Education Support Services have been working in an integrated way for years by automatically including work with the school, the family and wider services to provide support for "whole system change" as described in the LGA, DCSF and IDeA document Narrowing the Gap – July 2007.

Judging success

Success of Local Authority Services to schools tends to be judged in terms of proportions of pupils reaching expected levels at Key Stages 2 and 4, and Contextual Value Added. Accordingly the national profile of Gypsy Roma Traveller achievement looks like this.

● Gypsy Roma (national) ● Irish Traveller (national) ● All pupils (national)

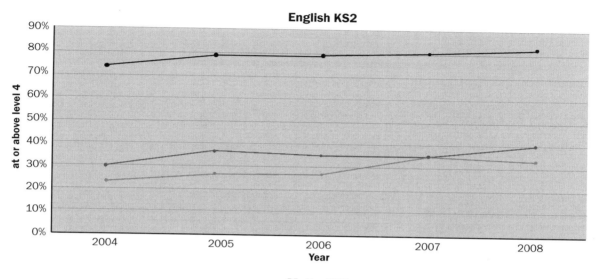

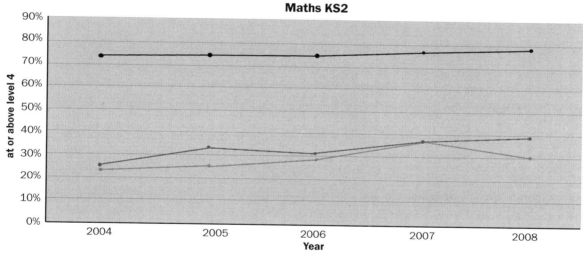

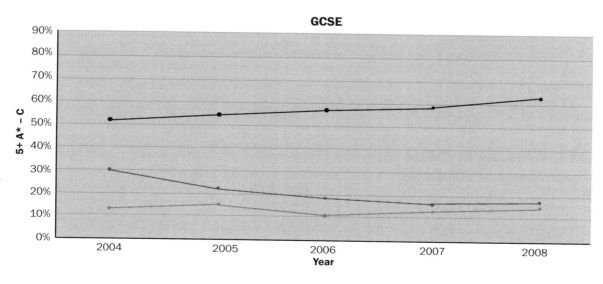

From these charts it might be assumed that Traveller Education Support Services have failed in their objective of raising the achievement of Gypsy Roma Traveller pupils. This implicit, and sometimes explicit, criticism has underpinned a number of national and local developments, seeking to critically evaluate the work of TESSs and bring them into line with other local authority services working with minority ethnic and vulnerable groups.

These graphs rightly cause concern, suggesting as they do that the gap of under-achievement between the Gypsy Roma Traveller cohorts and the rest of the population at Key Stage 2 is unlikely to close this century, and that the situation at GCSE is worse. The conclusion is being drawn that a policy of having dedicated TESSs has not been successful and alternatives need to be explored.

A better measure is Contextual Value Added, which indicates progress between two key stages. Although we cannot assume that Gypsy Roma Traveller pupils will have had continuity of education between two key stage tests, in practice they are more likely to have experienced continuity than those whose previous test scores are not available.

Ethnicity and Education, the DFES review of statistical data (2006), used their CVA model to compare progress between Key Stages 1 and 2 and Key Stages 2 and 4. The model makes it possible the isolate the effect of a particular characteristic (such as ethnicity) on attainment while controlling for other factors that impact upon attainment (such as prior attainment, gender, SEN status and deprivation).

"Most minority ethnic groups make more progress at school than similar White British pupils. ... However, there are still some ethnic groups who make less progress at primary school than White British pupils, even once prior attainment, deprivation and other factors are taken into account. These groups are Travellers of Irish Heritage, Gypsy/Roma, White & Black Caribbean (although the difference is minimal), Pakistani, Black Caribbean, any other Black background.
After the transition to secondary school, between Key Stages 2 to 4 all these groups except the two Traveller groups and the [mixed heritage] White & Black Caribbean group go on to make more progress than White British pupils with similar characteristics and levels of prior attainment."

Government concern about the underachievement of Gypsy Travellers was initiated by an Ofsted study *Raising the achievement of Minority Ethnic Pupils*, which focused on four groups: Bangladeshi, Black Caribbean, Pakistani and Gypsy Traveller backgrounds. It found Gypsy Travellers to be "most at risk in the education system". It is noticeable that two of the three other groups have negative CVA between Key Stages 1 and 2 but, apart from the Gypsy Roma Traveller groups, only mixed White and Black Caribbean have a small negative co-efficient between Key Stages 2 and 4.

Only pupils from the poorest areas defined on the Income Deprivation Affecting Children Index have lower CVA coefficients.[45]

Figure 1. Selected 2005 and 2004 Contextual Value Added Model Coefficients [45]

	2005		2004	
	Key Stage 1-2	**Key Stage 2-4**	**Key Stage 1-2**	**Key Stage 2-4**
Traveller of Irish Heritage	-0.50	-43.76	-0.68	-25.96
Gypsy/Roma	-0.38	-43.75	-0.79	-45.06
Any other white background	0.50	14.69	0.51	12.53
White and Black caribbean	-0.50	-1.26	-0.03	-0.53
Pakistani	-0.36	24.50	-0.25	27.06
Bangladeshi	0.26	30.93	0.28	32.09
Black Caribbean	-0.34	17.13	-0.30	15.04
Free School Meals	-0.4	-21.36	-0.40	-21.30
Pupils living in income deprived areas	-0.97	-65.14	-0.96	-65.09

From the table we might conclude:

The Primary Gypsy Roma Traveller pupils who have continuity of education between two key stages do not have serious Special Educational Needs, attend reasonably well and have a relatively stable home life will make similar progress to other children, although normally insufficient to close the gap. In the secondary phase, the situation is less positive.

In practice, however, this is a minority of children. Ethnicity and Education[47] presented data indicating that almost a quarter of Gypsy Roma Traveller pupils were at School Action Plus or had a statement of Special Education Need, double the proportion of any other ethnic minority group.

Figure 2. Percentage of Pupils with Special Educational Needs (School Action Plus/Statement) all schools 2004

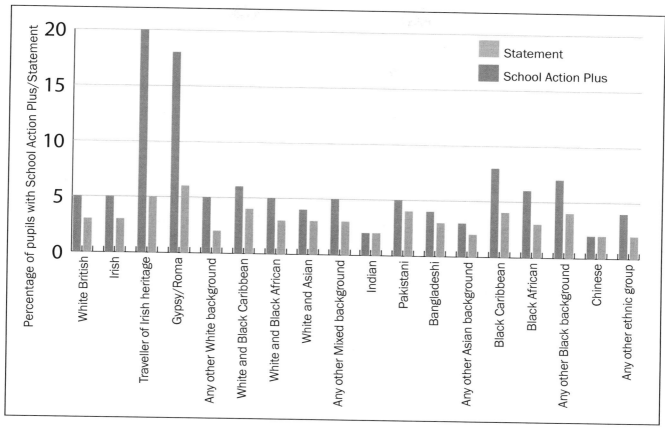

In many areas turnover rates are of the order of 40% and average time in the LA averages around two years. So the attainment of Gypsy Roma Travellers is more about Every Child Matters issues than about learning and teaching.

An international review of the impact of parental involvement and support on achievement[48] found that "in the primary age range the impact caused by different levels of parental involvement is much bigger than differences associated with variations in the quality of schools... Differences between parents in their level of involvement are associated with social class, poverty, health, and also with parental perception of their role and their levels of confidence in fulfilling it."

If we are committed to ensuring that Gypsy Roma Travellers enjoy and achieve, we have to approach their education within the context of their health, safety, economic well-being and social inclusion. TESSs have recognised this and an inter-agency approach has been a core principle of the work of most services.

It is important that the effectiveness of any provision is closely monitored and that the conclusions of evaluation be fed into policy. Unfortunately, however, we feel Traveller Education support is being judged against an inappropriate yardstick; one which fails to recognise the challenges involved in raising the achievement of vulnerable children from socially-excluded communities.

Exceeding the expected level can be anticipated as a result of a successful educational experience but, as we said in the Achievement section, there are many factors which can interfere with the process. Some may be under the control of the school and teachers (such as quality of teaching and learning), some may be a shared responsibility with the family and other agencies (such as attendance and health issues) and some may be completely beyond their control.

Just as personalisation is the key to making learning accessible, personalised monitoring is the key to evaluating the quality of education a pupil is receiving. Although it is subjective, it is possible to look at each child supported by the authority (this is where the relatively small numbers are a benefit) and ask the question "Is this child achieving his or her full potential?" For some families and children the fact that a child is in school is an achievement, and frequently the outcome of a great deal of effort by a TESS.

45 DCSF 2006

46 DSCF (2006).

47 DCSF (2005) Ethnicity and Education: The Evidence on Minority Ethnic Pupils Research Topic Paper: RTP01-05 p.22

48 Deforge, C (2003) The Impact of Parental Involvement, Parental Support and Family Education on Pupil Achievements and Adjustment: A Literature Review DfES Research Report RR433 p.4.

The number of Traveller children in school is a clear measure of the success of Traveller Education over the years. This has been a slow process, but in 1983 the DES issued a discussion paper which estimated that only 40% to 50% of Traveller children attended primary school. By 1996 Ofsted reported that there had been considerable success in improving attendance at the Primary phase, but the same report highlighted the difficulties in achieving transition to Secondary school. Personal experience tells us this is improving, with more pupils getting into both Key Stages 3 and 4 every year. But the whole community is not there yet. Looking at the pupil numbers used by the statisticians to collate the national tables, there continues to be significant under-representation of Traveller communities in the Secondary phase.

If a family is highly mobile, the speed of placement in school can be a key indicator of effectiveness. In the secondary phase, avoiding exclusion and drop out may be an achievement for the child and the school.

Having Special Educational Needs recognised and addressed may be important in ensuring a child is able to reach expected levels; for another child it may be recognition that it is not possible to reach such levels. The target needs to be personalised, and the assessment of whether any given level of achievement represents that child's potential is a matter of judgement.

In the case of highly mobile families, academic achievement may not be a realistic indicator of success; just remaining in contact and being in a position to support educational continuity if their circumstances change may be the most effective role to take. The safeguarding role of educational support services for Travellers cannot be over-estimated. Often TESS staff are the only frontline workers in day-to-day contact with families and they frequently draw safeguarding issues to the attention of other services. The network of TESSs often means that families receive continuity of support as they move from area to area, in a way that is much more difficult to achieve with area-based provision.

Here are some key performance indicators that could be used to indicate whether or not services supporting Traveller Education are having an impact.

Indicator	What is measured	Effectiveness of indicator
Target group	Number of Gypsy Roma Travellers 0-19 age group in the LA.	This will vary due to factors beyond the control of the service, but if numbers are growing there may be issues relating to availability of school places and levels of support given to schools and families.
Engagement	Proportion of cohorts engaged in educational settings and attending well.	This is an indicator of the effectiveness of the LA in including this marginalised group. Participation indicates the extent to which inclusion strategies are effective.
Mobility	Number of children arriving at or leaving an address over a period of time.	This is a contextual indicator; we are unlikely to be able to influence levels of mobility, but we should be aware of the magnitude of the challenge we face.
Pre-school engagement	Numbers of families contacted and proportion of pre-school children enrolled in settings.	Pre-school enrolment is voluntary, so 100% may not be a realistic target; the important thing is that families know the provision is available and any concerns and anxieties they have are addressed.
Parental participation	Parents attending parents' evenings, social functions, being employed or becoming Governors.	Deforge's study of the impact of parental participation and support for education suggests this could be a key indicator.
Response to mobility	Time elapsing between first visit and school enrolment.	This is a powerful indicator of the effectiveness of the authority in responding to the needs of transient families. Effective collaboration required between admissions, schools and families.

Attendance	Possible sessions, authorised, unauthorised absence and reason for absence.	Attendance needs to be treated as an indicator of lack of inclusion, health issues, safety fears and financial issues.
Pupil progress	Termly pupil tracking records.	Achievement needs to be monitored at more frequent intervals than the end of key stages to ensure pupils are getting appropriate levels of intervention, SEN and EAL support.
Transitions	Proportion of key stage cohort transferring successfully.	Indicator of effectiveness of transition arrangements outlined in Transitions section.
Exclusions	Number of exclusions, sessions excluded, reason and SEN collected each term.	How effective is the authority in finding alternatives to exclusion where exclusion can increase vulnerability and play into the hands of students who are resistant to attending school?
Post 16 outcomes	Number of Year 12 cohort in education, training or employment (including self-employment).	Traveller education support continues beyond statutory school age. More young people are continuing in education and training as well as entering employment. This may be a more appropriate indicator than 5+ A*-C at GCSE.

What can we do?

The aim of this book has been to provide a background introduction to the issues impacting on the education of Gypsy Roma Travellers. It should be clear from the preceding chapters that we believe that only if education is viewed within the Every Child Matters context, will it be possible to address the shocking levels of under-achievement, low attendance, high exclusion and SEN identification. Here we list, for practitioners with a role to play in this process, three suggestions of steps you could take to ensure that you or your service responds appropriately to these communities. It may be you are already doing these things, in which case you will probably be in a position to think of alternatives to take you on to the next level.

Director of Children's Services	Allocate one day per year to develop your own understanding of these groups and the challenges they face, eg, read a book, attend a conference.	Use Gypsy Roma Traveller groups as a litmus test for effective inter-agency working; ask policy makers and practitioners, "What will the impact be on Gypsy Roma Traveller communities?"	Develop inter-agency links, supported by training, to ensure that you build an effective corporate response to needs across the ECM agenda and beyond.
Chief Education Officer/Assistant Director Children Families and Schools	Ensure that an appropriate person in your Senior Management team has responsibility for this area and keeps you updated on issues.	Be aware of progress against key indicators for all known Gypsy Roma Traveller pupils (not only those defined by census categories) and the strategies being employed to Narrow the Gap.	Build the capacity of LA staff and schools to include Gypsy Roma Travellers in development of Community Cohesion policies.
Director of Social Services/ Assistant Director - Safeguarding	Develop effective inter-agency links with colleagues in education, voluntary sector and housing services.	Identify, share and develop expertise within the directorate; ensure training provided to new staff includes background information on Gypsy Roma Traveller communities.	Develop clear policy on safeguarding issues with cultural components, such as under-age marriage, child employment, highly mobile children at risk.
Head of school improvement and standards	Ensure all advisers are aware of how their specialist area can impact on Gypsy Roma Travellers and communicate it to schools.	Ensure that your division has a productive relationship with Traveller Education professionals, mainstreaming their expertise.	Ensure that School Improvement Partners are aware of the issues for Gypsy Roma Traveller communities and the schools supporting them so that high quality support is in place.
Head of education welfare, inclusion and attendance	Have a clear, working relationship with Traveller Education professionals to improve Gypsy Roma Traveller attendance, prevent drop out and cope with mobility.	Organise partnership meetings where your frontline staff, Traveller Education staff and colleagues engaged in Behaviour and Attendance strategies can develop shared understanding and co-ordinate approaches.	Ensure staff are aware of appropriate use of "T" absence code, 200 day rule, dual registration arrangements and Elective Home Education registration.
Head of admissions	Audit your systems to ensure they support fair and speedy access for mid-term arrivals.	Build the capacity of frontline staff to respond appropriately to families who are unfamiliar with the education system.	Offer training to school-based staff on culturally sensitive enrolment procedures.
Strategy managers	Be clear in your own mind how each of the strategy strands you manage can include and benefit Gypsy Roma Traveller pupils.	Ensure that consultants emphasise the potential of various interventions to make the curriculum accessible to Gypsy Roma Traveller pupils and help narrow the gap of underachievement.	Develop good partnerships working with Traveller Education professionals around recognition of culture, identity, learning styles and relevance.

Traveller Education Support Service Coordinator	Build capacity through partnership working with families, schools, LA and the voluntary sector. Make sure your service contributions are spread fairly (not necessarily equally) across all families, schools and agencies in your area.	Safeguard and develop the skills of TESS staff. Make sure you and they are up-to-date with developments and have career options. Create opportunities for community members to enter the education workforce.	Find an appropriate balance between being responsive and reflective. Move along the continuum safety net -> sticking plaster -> scaffolding -> structural response.
Traveller Education Staff	Help families become independent users of the education system and schools to have independent relationships with families.	Talk the talk. Understand the issues class teachers are grappling with, then find ways of relating their priorities to include Gypsy Roma Traveller pupils.	Don't allow yourself to become marginalised. Critically evaluate your impact. Identify ways you could be more effective and try to implement them. Have developmental projects in your workload and allocate time to them.
Headteachers	Run a welcoming, inclusive school, with clear, realistic expectations and effective personalisation including Distance Learning.	Prioritise the engagement of hard-to-reach parents, reassuring them about safety, morality and identity, creating opportunities to contribute to an ethos of understanding and respect.	Recognise the school's role in promoting community cohesion and challenging racism. Include Gypsy Roma Traveller communities in policies and practice and record this in the school's self-evaluation.
Subject leaders	Make the curriculum relevant, practical and enjoyable.	Incorporate the knowledge, skills and ways of thinking that Gypsy Roma and Traveller pupils bring to the school environment.	Encourage community engagement in projects and celebrations.
Class teachers	Ensure that pupils admitted in mid-year are made to feel welcome and that their individual needs are assessed.	Personalise the curriculum for Gypsy Roma Traveller pupils as for all pupils.	Be vigilant in noticing how Gypsy Roma Traveller pupils are being included socially in the class group and check that they are not isolated.
Ethnic Minority achievement staff	Work collaboratively with TESSs where there are language issues for Gypsy Roma Traveller pupils.	When you are offering training on Minority Ethnic achievement, don't forget the Gypsy Roma Traveller community. Invite your local TESS to contribute.	Read significant publications on the education of Gypsy Roma Traveller pupils, and reflect on how the issues raised can be included in your practice.
SENCO	Ensure that your school's achievement data is monitored by ethnic group. Is there a good spread of achievement across the Gypsy Roma Traveller pupils or is the achievement depressed for this group? Reflect on the proportion of Gypsy Roma Traveller pupils in your school on the Code of Practice. Is it disproportionate? Are the assessments correct?	Review the IEPs for Gypsy Roma Traveller pupils with Special Needs. Is there a cultural component to their difficulties? Does the IEP take account of this in a positive way? Do you provide support for Distance Learners on the code of practice?	How are teachers providing personalised learning for Gypsy Roma Traveller pupils? Does this include Distance Learning where appropriate? Consider whether the parents of Gypsy Roma Traveller pupils with Special Needs fully understand and support the process. Are you making maximum use of their contribution?

Inclusion Officer	Check that policies in schools are Equality Impact Assessed and regularly monitored. Unpick Gypsy Roma Traveller attendance patterns and provide appropriate support to address poor attendance. What inter-agency strategies could improve this area of work?	Prioritise training that raises the issues and barriers to Gypsy Roma Traveller inclusion. Make sure parents understand how attendance underpins achievement. Be creative in engaging them with the work of the school. Strike a balance between high expectations and cultural sensitivity. Is the information they need given to them at the induction meeting?	What is the connection between accommodation and education for Gypsy Roma Traveller pupils in your area? What inter-agency strategies could bring about improvements? Prioritise training that raises the issues and barriers to Gypsy Roma Traveller inclusion.
Teaching assistant	Ensure that Gypsy Roma Traveller children are made welcome and are included in social groups. Use your relationship to identify interests, learning styles and any concerns the pupils have. Communicate them to the teacher.	Make time to talk to parents and show them the good work the children have been doing in school.	Check how the Gypsy Roma Traveller pupils are coping at lunch times and break times. Are they included in social groups? Try to find opportunities to raise issues of culture and identity in small group work. Make sure questions are open so children are encouraged to link education to their home lives.
Parent	Talk to the school as you want them to talk to you. Tell them what they need to know to get the best out of your child. Contact them straight away if anything is concerning you. Praise them when they do well.	Help the school develop its understanding of your way of life traditions and skills. Take part in the social life of the school, go on school journeys and go to parents' evenings. Volunteer as a helper or as a school governor.	If you are going to go travelling let the school know in good time and, if you can, give a return date. Contact them if your plans change. Make sure your children attend regularly when you aren't travelling.
Voluntary organisations	Does your organisation do outreach work? This "hard-to- reach" community becomes accessible if visited at home. Build capacity among the communities to make education providers take account of their identities and cultures.	There are many opportunities for voluntary organisations to support the Gypsy Roma Traveller community at this time. Support with developing activities for Gypsy Roma Traveller History Month would be very welcome. Share the objectives of your work with statutory agencies, clarifying where you work, who you work with, and what falls within and outside your remit. Contribute to effective inter-agency policies and practice.	Gypsy Roma Traveller communities vary greatly in their levels of wealth. While some communities are very poor, others are wealthy and highly self-sufficient. Ensure that your offer fits with the needs of the community. Develop training and employment pathways to develop the skills of community members to increase their representation in the workforce
Personal/careers advisor	Ensure that you have had good training about the issues that affect the Gypsy Roma Traveller community.	Many young people from Gypsy Roma Traveller communities aspire to self-employment. You will need to keep this in mind when offering advice.	Share advice given with the local TESS so they can engage in joint working and skill sharing.

Relevant Legislation

Attendance

Education Act 1996.
Section 444 of the Act states that:

"If a child of compulsory school age who is a registered pupil at a school fails to attend regularly at the school, the parent of the child is guilty of an offence."

However, the Section goes on to identify circumstances in which the parent of a child who has "no fixed abode" is protected from conviction for the non-attendance of their children at school where it can be demonstrated:

- that he is engaged in a trade or business of such a nature as to require him to travel from place to place,

- that the child has attended at a school as a registered pupil as regularly as the nature of that trade or business permits, and

- if the child has attained the age of six years, that he has made at least two hundred attendances during the period of twelve months ending with the date on which the proceedings were instituted.

This legislation is designed to protect Traveller parents from unreasonable prosecution for their child's non-attendance at school. However, it does not mean that part-time education for Traveller children is legally acceptable: 200 sessions should be regarded as the minimum.

Community Cohesion

From September 2007 schools have been under a new duty to promote community cohesion. This duty springs, at least in part, from the Equality Act of 2006, which established the Commission for Equality and Human Rights. This legislation brought together the monitoring of the:

- Sex Discrimination Act 1975

- Race Relations Act 1976 as amended in 2000

- Disability Discrimination Act 1995 as amended in 2005

- Human Rights Act 1998

- Equal Pay Act

- Equality Act (Sexual Orientation) Regulations

- Equality Act (Gender realignment) Regulations

- Special Needs and Disability Act

- Employment Equality (Religion or Belief) regulations 2003

The outcome for schools was:

The Education and Inspections Act 2006 (Duty to Promote Community Cohesion)
The Duty to Promote Community Cohesion requires the school to have policies to promote equality, which can take the form of either a 'single equality policy' or a number of individual policies that cover each of the areas of Race, Gender, Sexual Orientation, Disability, Religion and Belief, Employment and Human Rights.

Human Rights

The Human Rights Act 1998.
This Act came fully into force in October 2000. The Human Rights Act 1998 embeds the European Convention on Human Rights in UK law. These rights not only impact matters of life and death, they also affect the rights one has in everyday life: what can be said and done, one's beliefs, the right to a fair trial and other similar basic entitlements.

Most rights have limits to ensure that they do not unfairly damage other people's rights. However, certain rights, such as the right not to be tortured, may not be limited by a court or anybody else.

There is a responsibility to respect the rights of others and an expectation that the rights of all will be respected.

Human rights are the following:
- The right to life

- Freedom from torture and degrading treatment

- Freedom from slavery and forced labour

- The right to liberty

- The right to a fair trial

- The right not to be punished for something that wasn't a crime when you did it

- The right to respect for private and family life

- Freedom of thought, conscience and religion, and freedom to express your beliefs

- Freedom of expression

- Freedom of assembly and association

- The right to marry and to start a family

- The right not to be discriminated against in respect of these rights and freedoms

- The right to peaceful enjoyment of your property

- The right to an education

- The right to participate in free elections

- The right not to be subjected to the death penalty

The Human Rights Act has been most frequently used by the Gypsy Roma Traveller community when submitting planning applications to develop sites into living accommodation where a number of rights, including the Right to an Education, have been quoted.

Local Authority Duty

1944 Education Act as amended in 1981 and 1996.

The Education Act 1996 places local authorities under a statutory duty to ensure that education is available for all school age children in their area, appropriate to their age, ability and aptitude, and any special education needs they may have.

Circular 1/81 emphasizes this duty extends to all children residing in their area, whether permanently or temporarily. It thus embraces in particular Traveller children, including Gypsies.

The Children Act 2004.

This Act puts into law the proposals set out in the Green Paper Every Child Matters. It creates a clear accountability for Children's Services, enables better joint working, and revises and strengthens the local authority role in safeguarding children.

The Education and Inspection Act 2006.

This Act introduced a new relationship between local authorities and schools. Local authorities are required to appoint School Improvement Partners to support and challenge headteachers and school governors, helping them to focus on priorities and targets for school improvement. It also creates a new strategic role for local authorities in the establishment, closure or alteration of schools and the development of Trust schools.

In addition it set out changes to:
- The admissions framework to ensure fair access to schools

- The entitlement of 14-19 year olds to 14 new diploma courses

- School Transport

- School behaviour policies

- Ofsted inspections

Parental Duty

Education Act 1996 Section 7.

It shall be the duty of the parent of every child of compulsory school age to cause him to receive efficient full-time education suitable to his age, ability and aptitude and to any special educational needs either by regular school attendance or otherwise.

Race Equality

Race Relations Act 1976 (Amended 2000).

The Race Relations (Amendment) Act 2000, and subsequent regulations enacted in 2001, requires local authorities to promote race equality through a general duty. The general duty requires authorities to:
- Eliminate unlawful racial discrimination

- Promote equal opportunities

- Promote good relations between people from different racial groups.

The Race Relations (Amendment) Act places specific duties on schools to enable them to comply with the general duty. The general duty applies to all public bodies and requires them to promote race equality. In addition, each school must have
- A written race equality policy and arrangements for assessing and monitoring its effectiveness.

- Schools are also required to monitor the operation of their policies on their pupils, parents and staff, particularly with regard to the achievement of minority ethnic pupils, including those from Gypsy Roma and Travellers of Irish Heritage backgrounds.

There is a requirement to review how the school's assessment and implementation of policy affect the attainment levels of these pupils. Schools are also required to take reasonable practical steps to make available the results of the monitoring.

Equality Act 2006.

This Act brought together the commission for Racial Equality, the Equal Opportunities Commission and the Disability Rights Commission, replacing them with a single Equality and Human Rights Commission. This legislation was introduced as a precursor to a promised Single Equality Act. The Equality Bill was published on 27th April 2009. If this Bill is passed before a general election is held, it is expected to come into force in Autumn 2010. If passed, this law proposes to extend, simplify and harmonise existing legislation.

Rights of the Child

The Children Act 1989.

This Act brought the UK closer to the objectives of the UN convention on the rights of the child and requires local authorities to provide a range of services to children in need. In particular they have a general duty to safeguard and promote the welfare of children in need within the area. There is a particular requirement to work in partnership with parents.

The UN Convention on the Rights of the child.

The UN General Assembly adopted this convention on the 20th November 1989. It recognises that children need special care and protection and that the family is the main form of protection for children. It recognises the need for legal protection before and after birth and the importance of respecting the cultural values of the child's community.

Conclusion

Community Development

Over the last 25 years there has been significant progress in advancing the education of Gypsy Roma Traveller pupils, but there remains a very long way to go; particularly if we use attainment in national tests as the only yard-stick. We have tried to show how much progress has been made, but also the range of challenges, which explains why education alone cannot compensate for the extremes of racism and social exclusion experienced by so many families.

Much of this progress was made before mainstreaming and can be mainly attributed to the partnership between schools, families and TESSs. We can show real and sustained progress based on core funding that has been granted rather than on short-term funding-led projects which can cause fluctuations in results. Children who accessed education in the 1980s and '90s are now parents themselves and are familiar with schools and the processes that TESSs employ. In many ways they are better consumers of education than their parents were; they know some of the pitfalls and the questions to ask. Schools are more familiar and less daunting places to them.

Those who had good experiences in the past can have a very positive attitude and clear views about the benefits of education. Now, it is not unusual to find members of the communities accessing education independently and working in schools as Learning Support Assistants. Before long community members will qualify as teachers who are proud to declare their ethnicity. We know that there are Gypsy Roma Travellers who are already qualified teachers but it is still unusual for them to openly declare their ethnicity.

More children from Gypsy Roma Traveller backgrounds are successfully accessing education at all phases from Early Years through to Further and Higher Education. Their progress is tracked from Foundation Stage through to GCSE, but their ability to sustain full-time attendance and enrolment for the whole of the statutory period is very variable and also needs to be closely monitored. Not only do the figures need to be collected, but they need to be analysed and the underlying causes addressed. We still need to improve community confidence in the value of Ethnic Monitoring and thus ensure that all the children who do attend settings and schools are monitored to improve attainment and celebrate success.

However, where experiences have been poor and today's parents have suffered marginalisation and discrimination or have attended school but not learned even the basic skills, attitudes towards education can be hostile and difficult to challenge. There is still work to be done within Gypsy Roma Traveller communities to build confidence in

- the value of education to their communities, especially culturally relevant vocational education for the 14-19 phase

- the safety of children, both in school and travelling to and from school

- professionals' ability to design courses which give continuity to mobile pupils

- the benefits of declaring their ethnicity

- official capacity to identify and allocate sufficient living accommodation to support regular school attendance

- the ability of educational establishments to provide courses which enable their children to catch-up on missed work.

There need to be staff, within a mainstream service, with these issues high on their job descriptions if the foundations laid over the past decades are to be built upon.

Mainstreaming

We have always aspired to secure unhindered access to mainstream education for Traveller pupils; in fact, we often used it as a measure of our success. We still say that when Gypsy Roma Traveller pupils can access education of their own accord, unhindered by racism, and achieve similar outcomes to their settled peers our work will be done. As this will mean we live in a fairer and more equal society we strongly desire that at a future date TESSs will no longer be needed and the work we do will become obsolete. However, that day is not here yet, and current moves towards mainstreaming and integrated working offer the opportunity to move towards greater flexibility and sensitivity in provision. So long as this is done carefully and with a light touch to ensure that all the progress made so far is absorbed into the new ways of working, then all should be well.

The danger is that, in the imperative to introduce integrated, inter-agency working there will be insufficient time for local authority strategic planners to absorb the complexity of Traveller Education expertise from practitioners who may seem to be making apparently self-serving arguments for retaining their current ways of working. The push to raise attainment at key stages could be prioritised over the wider ECM need to promote access and engagement and consequently much of the work of TESSs could be seen to be irrelevant, or even counter-productive.

In fact, the breadth of practice within TESSs could be used as a model for providing the wrap-around provision envisaged by the CAF, Every Child Matters, NFER Narrowing the Gap, and the Extra Mile documents, all of which highlight the need to make progress on all fronts and not simply on pupil attainment. We would argue that all the pupils who have been identified as vulnerable to failure in the education system need access to a Narrowing the Gap approach to their development, working across departments and agencies. Rather than constraining TESSs within Pupil Achievement Services, it may be more productive to look in depth at the work of TESS to see how their practice could enhance the achievement of all.

Safeguarding

The UN Convention on the Rights of the Child recognises that children need special care and protection and that the family is the main form of protection for children. It recognises the need for legal protection and the importance of respect for the cultural values of the child's community.

We have legislation and guidance to ensure that children are kept safe within our society, but most of this relies on the children and families being in touch with health professionals, schools, early years settings or similar. Contact with these practitioners can be problematic for Traveller families.

TESSs provide an important safeguarding function in accessing pupils to education and ensuring that pupils resident in the local authority are known and enrolled in school or registered for EHE. Their role in ensuring that children do not withdraw from the education system by going travelling and never returning to school, even when they return to the local authority, assists the Local Authority to ensure that all children are offered similar levels of protection.

Funding

The loss of ring-fenced funding represents the greatest threat to Traveller Education Services in recent years. While we understand the Government's desire to decentralise and ensure that there is the ability to make good local decisions, it is clear that this decision has undermined the work and even the existence of Traveller Education support.

Our concerns are that it would not be difficult for local authorities to withdraw TESS support into an "advice for schools" model supported by Education Welfare in the belief that this would cover all the bases

and possibly save money. Ethnic monitoring would show the number of children accessing education. Attainment and attendance would improve as schools build their relationships with their Gypsy Roma Traveller families. Schools and local authorities would still need to set targets for the achievement of Gypsy Roma Traveller pupils and the DCSF would report on these. However, it is the most vulnerable children and families who would suffer: the highly mobile, the newly-arrived, the excluded and self-excluding who are currently engaged and kept on track by highly-focussed and targeted community outreach work being undertaken by TESSs. Who would ensure that families are aware of Children's Centre provision, nursery places and schools with available places? Who would signpost parenting support or housing advice? Who would re-engage 16 year olds who have been Home Educated? Who would plan Gypsy Roma Traveller Month, engage Romanes interpreters, identify role models and create opportunities for community employment? Who would keep track when a family lives in one LA, sends their children to schools in another, and there are Special Education Needs issues?

Those who argue that specialist Traveller Education support is anachronistic may identify mainstream staff who could take on these and the other roles, but we would argue that, in our experience, to add additional responsibilities to already onerous job descriptions does not ensure the job gets done; it only ensures there is someone to blame when it doesn't get done. Supporting the access to education and opportunities of the most marginal families is very time-consuming; it requires commitment and persistence, and that is far more likely to be found within a dedicated team of professionals with an interest in the communities and their cultures, than as an unwanted addition to the workload of a generic team.

Concern about the education of Travellers has long been a national issue rather than a local one. While the DCSF commissions the National Strategies to undertake a Gypsy Roma Traveller Achievement programme and commissions studies into the causes of underachievement, local concern rarely goes beyond the Local Authority TESS and Gypsy Liaison Officer. This is because numbers are relatively small, the communities are mobile and from a political point of view the topic is controversial.

We would hold that an urgent review of Traveller Education funding is necessary because:
1. The issue of the underachievement of Traveller pupils is a national concern.

2. The numbers in school in individual authorities are frequently too small and levels of staff awareness too limited for sufficient priority to be given in local planning and implementation to the ECM needs of these communities.

3. All current reporting of progress in Traveller Education to the DCSF is summative of events in school, so that local authorities who do not get Traveller pupils into school suffer no penalty.

In the light of this, ring-fenced funding measuring the ability of a local authority to access pupils to education would concentrate minds to look carefully at admissions and transport issues. If it included a count of pupils out of school, questioned the lack of living accommodation in different local authorities, looked at community involvement and levels of mobility as well as pupil achievement, local authorities would gain a greater overall level of ownership of these issues. We see this as similar to the way in which the National Strategies-funded schools took on greater ownership of wider Gypsy Roma Traveller issues through their participation in the programme.

However, the funding needs to be sustained until the results are almost universal. Great progress has been made with small funding granted to TESSs but Traveller Education practitioners know that short term 'project based' funding raises expectations, creates false hope and can undermine the progress that has already been made. One of the joys of e-Lamp funding is that it has been sustained for sufficiently long to enable the strategies to be embedded and year on year development to be sustained.

Educating Gypsy Roma Traveller pupils is a measure of our ability as a society to ensure that we have the capacity to deliver a basic human right to all our citizens. There is a duty to ensure that public prejudice and media hostility, combined with inflexibilities within the education system, do not prevent these children from receiving an entitlement that will enable them to be active and productive members of their own communities and society at large. This requires and deserves sustained national ring-fenced funding.

Gypsy Roma Travellers History Month

The way of life of many Gypsy Roma Travellers has changed radically over the past twenty-five years, not always for the better. At each step along the way, Traveller Education professionals have sought to optimise the educational outcomes and make the most of any opportunities provided. Gypsy Roma Traveller History Month (which has grown from an educational initiative) is showing, in its second year, the potential to change the way society and the communities think about and celebrate culture and history.

The first year was remarkably successful, taking account of the short lead time and a general uncertainty about how it would be received, but the second not only transcended some of the tensions and anxieties of the first, but also went on to become a genuinely community-owned event. The launch at Westminster was an intercultural celebration, where Gypsies and Roma explored their shared heritage and language, while music united all the communities and generations. The discovery, by an English Gypsy, that her family had been sold into slavery in America starkly illustrated how the oral and family history may lead to a rewriting of national history and create powerful alliances with Roma and other enslaved communities. It felt as though the pride which we know exists in Gypsy Roma Traveller identity and culture, had become available to be shared within the communities, with schools and with society.

This brave step, carefully planned and implemented by community members and Traveller Education professionals at national and local levels, seemed to elicit a matching response from schools, libraries, council departments and the voluntary sector. If the press sniped, no-one paid attention. Children in schools, apprehensive about having the spotlight turned on them, were surprised and pleased to find that other children showed real interest in aspects of their culture. They told stories and made films, shared photos and made artwork.

TESSs put huge amounts of time into planning and organising events, even to the detriment of the day job and their social lives, but most would agree it was time well spent. The profiles of the communities, and the TESSs, were raised in an unexpected and positive way, contributing to a positive and affirmative ethos in schools and authorities.

Those who see no need for TESSs, may look at the role they have taken in making the most of the opportunity presented by the Month and ask themselves, "Could this have happened if TESS functions were devolved across the authority?" and "Isn't this an excellent example of mainstreaming in action?"

In 2009 there was a feeling of a step-change in our way of working, with everyone pulling together and everyone wanting to get in on the act. It wasn't furtive, defensive or cautious; it was loud and proud. The communities were leading, mainstream services were responding positively and TESSs were facilitating. This is mainstreaming in action and the model on which to develop our work.

APPENDIX 1

Gypsy Traveller Education Service
Transition checklist

Student		DoB	
Address		Home phone	
Primary School		School phone	
Secondary school		School phone	

September	Preparation	Contact admissions, order prospectus, establish timetable.	
		May include Catholic, out-of-borough and City academies which may have different timetables.	
	Identify cohort and schools	Take account of siblings, friendship groups and SEN issues.	
		Take account of proximity, faith and ethos.	
	Family visits	Select viable group of schools to suggest to each family.	
		Establish programme of open days.	
		Share Secondary school book with families.	
		Visit to make sure families understand process, timetable and responsibilities.	
October	Reminders	Emphasise importance of choice and timing to get an appropriate place.	
		Encourage school visits, accompany if necessary.	
		Establish whether there are literacy issues, social concerns or resistance to transfer.	
		Mention Ethnic Monitoring categories and purpose, including monitoring of racist incidents.	
		Establish whether family is comfortable with TESS involvement.	
		Contact schools or families during last week before deadline.	
		Contact school to ask for letters to family to be copied to TESS where appropriate (literacy difficulties).	
	Check	Final check with primary school to make sure forms have been returned.	
January	Interview/visit support	Remind or accompany families to interviews.	
		Visit families, establish whether they are happy with allocation.	
March	Check allocations	Take appropriate action if family not satisfied.	
		Involve parents if possible.	
May/June	Support Primary school visits to secondary schools	Arrange individual visits if Primary school is not normal feeder (may be necessary with Catholic and out-of-borough schools).	
		Discuss uniform and equipment requirements with parents.	

July	Family visit	Provide financial assistance where necessary.	
		Establish if school has uniform stock.	
	School visit	Establish arrangements for first day and make sure family is aware.	
		Alert school to TESS involvement, stress importance of transition support and early warning of breakdown.	
		Identify learning support issues or behaviour of which school may need to be aware.	
September	Enrolment	Monitor and support enrolment.	
		Make arrangements with school to monitor and support inclusion.	

APPENDIX II

Protocol for supporting access and attendance of Gypsy Roma Traveller children in school

Gypsy Traveller families living in or visiting the area include families of Irish Traveller, English and Eastern European Roma, Circus Fairground and New Traveller heritages. These communities face racism and social exclusion which may make them reluctant to send their children to school or prevent them from benefiting from educational provision; the educational experiences of many Gypsy Traveller parents have been inadequate or unsatisfactory.

The Education Welfare Service has a statutory responsibility to ensure that parents comply with the legal requirement that they educate their children. The Traveller Education Service does not have a statutory duty to enforce attendance and therefore works with families by consent, providing information, advice and encouragement. This protocol describes how the two services will work together.

Newly arrived families

1. Both services will inform each other if they become aware of a Gypsy Traveller family at a new address (which may be an unauthorised camp, an official site or any form of housing) within the borough.

2. Normally the TESS will make the first approach to the family to establish whether there are school-age children in the family, whether they are currently in school and whether the family requires support in finding school places.

3. The TESS will continue to work with the family until the children start attending school and will inform the EWS of the placements made or the reasons for any delays in the process.

4. Where families are living on unauthorised camps the TESS and EWS should arrange to make an initial joint visit as soon as practicable after the establishment of the camp, in order to establish the educational needs of the families living there.

Resistant families

1. If the family is resistant to school placement and is not arranging for education otherwise, the TESS should inform EWS who will take appropriate action to secure attendance.

2. TESS and EWS should meet each term to review lists of school-age children out of school and identify any cases where the TESS feel unable to make further progress; lead responsibility should then revert to the EWS.

3. In cases where the EWS has initiated legal proceedings to secure attendance, the TESS will remain available to the family in a supportive role if they are minded to seek school placements.

4. Decisions about prosecution for failure to enrol will be taken by the EWS, taking into account any representations which the TESS might make. Prosecutions should only be initiated in cases where there is a reasonable expectation that they will lead to school attendance.

Attendance issues

1. If a Gypsy Traveller child fails to attend school without a reason being given, the matter should be followed up by the school and EWS as in the case of all other children.

2. The TESS should be given the opportunity to provide additional information about family circumstances and address any issues which might be preventing school attendance.

3. Decisions about prosecution will be taken by the EWS, taking into account any representations which the TESS might make. Prosecutions should only be initiated in cases where there is a reasonable expectation that they will lead to improved attendance.

4. Gypsy Traveller communities are dispersed over wide geographical areas and maintain cultural integrity through celebrations such as weddings, christenings and funerals, as well as visits to horse fairs and religious gatherings. EWS and TESS will work together to provide information and training to develop sensitivity to cultural issues which may impact on attendance.

5. Poor attendance can be linked to issues of inclusion and attainment. The TESS will work with schools to help them develop policies which include children from diverse backgrounds, combat racism against

Gypsy Travellers and build mutual respect between children from different cultural groups. The TESS will also provide support to schools in differentiating the curriculum, and supporting access to an alternative curriculum where appropriate.

Mobility issues

- If children cease attending, school should inform the EWS in the first instance. If the family have left a forwarding address, the EWS should attempt to verify that the children are placed in school before authorising their removal from the school roll.

- If the family does not provide a forwarding address, or if the EWS fails to make contact with the family at the address given, the TESS should be given the opportunity to establish where the family is living and whether the children have enrolled in another school. The child should only be taken off roll when TESS and ESW agree that all reasonable efforts to trace the family have been made and no further enquiries are possible.

- Where families wish to travel for a part of the year they can ask the headteacher to authorise a "Traveller" absence, marked in the register as a "T". This is at the discretion of the headteacher, but should be encouraged as a means of making education compatible with a nomadic lifestyle. Families should be encouraged to give an estimated return date and asked to make telephone contact by that date if their return is delayed. If families decide not to return, they should be encouraged to let the school know as soon as practicable. Where travelling families fail to return or contact the school, the TESS and EWS should have the opportunity to trace the family before they are taken off roll.

- The TESS will try to maintain educational continuity for mobile Travellers by trying to identify previous schools and by making contact with TESSs in the areas to which they move. This process is particularly important with families who move a great deal, including those on unauthorised camps, circuses and fairgrounds.

- Where children from unauthorised camps are attending schools, they should not be automatically taken off roll when the camp is evicted. Families may stay in the area and choose to bring their children back to the school. The procedure for these children should be the same as for any other Traveller family changing address.

Glossary

ACERT	Advisory Council for the Education of Romanies and other Travellers
AfL	Assessment for Learning
APP	Assessing Pupil Performance
CAF	Common Assessment Framework
CPD	Continuing Professional Development
CRE	Commission for Race Equality
DCSF (formerly DfES)	Department of Children, Schools and Families (formerly Department for Education and Science)
EAL	English as an Additional Language
ECM	Every Child Matters
EHE	Elective Home Education
EHRC	Equality and Human Rights Commission
E-lamp	E-Learning And Mobility Project
EO	Education Otherwise
EU	European Union
EWS	Education Welfare Service
FSM	Free School Meals eligibility
IEP	Individual Education Plan
LA	Local Authority
NATT+	National Association of Teachers for Travellers + other professionals
SEAL	Social and Emotional Aspects of Learning
SEN	Special Education Needs
SLT	Senior Leadership Team
TE[S]S	Traveller Education [Support] Service
VAT	Value Added Tax
VCG	Vulnerable Children Grant
WIRT	Traveller of Irish Heritage
WROM	Gypsy Roma ethnic code

Notes

Notes

Notes

Notes